GHOSTS
AND
WITCHES

J. Wentworth Day

Illustrated by
Michael Ayrton

Dorset Press
New York

This edition published by Dorset Press,
a division of Marboro Books Corp.
1991 Dorset Press

ISBN 0-88029-730-1

Printed and bound in the United States of America

M 9 8 7 6 5 4 3 2 1

CONTENTS

CONTENTS

Introduction

WHAT a gallimaufry of ghosts and medievalism is in this old Suffolk forest of trees more ancient than time—and for that matter, what a gallimaufry of ghosts is about us wherever we walk in the older parts of England. That is, of course, if we have the sense to hear and see a little further than our material noses."

It is not so many years since that recondite scholar with the gay wit and embracing Christianity, the late Dr. Montague Rendall, one-time Headmaster of Winchester, made that remark to me as we walked together on an enchanted September afternoon of sunlight and golden silence, in that Hans Andersen wood of the old gods, Staverton Forest, which lies at the door of the grey magnificence of the old gatehouse of Butley Priory on the Suffolk coast, where "Monty" Rendall lived the last happy years of his life in classic peace.

That old and haunted wood of ancient trees was a place sacred before Christ walked on Galilee, a place of which I have written elsewhere "so old that its memories are for-gotten, its old gods blown whispers down the aisles of an older Britain that died when the Romans came".

And amid that mysticism of old trees so grotesquely beautiful that they are almost frightening, we talked of ghosts and the strange and ancient beliefs that are part of the weft of English history—an unearthly pattern woven, sometimes enchantingly and sometimes forbiddingly, into that immemorial background of inherited traditions which is the heritage of the countryside, the ultimate mother of all men, whether of town or village.

So, in this book, I have collected together a gallimaufry of ghosts and a web of witches. For the most part they are stories heard at first hand, or stories sent to me in reply to letters which I wrote to many provincial newspapers. Indeed, the replies to my letters would have filled not one book, but two, and the strange thing is that all, or most of them, bore the undeniable stamp of authenticity. The writers clearly and honestly believed the truth, or at any rate half the truth, of the things they had seen or the tales they had heard.

That, perhaps, is how most of us regard ghost stories. We hesitate to believe them wholeheartedly—but we never hesi-tate to listen or to retail the tales we are told. I do not pre-tend to be a spiritualist. I dabble in no demonology and despise the diseased minds which grope after the Black Arts. But there is a fascination about the legends of the countryside which is undeniable, irresistible, and probably indestructible.

I confess that I have sat up hopefully, on dark nights and moonlight nights, in haunted houses, old and new. I have walked through spectral woods when owls hooted and bats flew. I have been on desolate seaward marshes at midnight, where the corpse candles glow and have waded through noisome fens where bitterns boomed and Wills-o'-the-Wisp flit their lambent course. But, with the exception of that one extraordinary war-time vision of a ghostly cavalry skirmish,

to the truth of which I would affirm most solemnly, I have
seen no ghosts.

True, no power would have coaxed me upstairs to the
dark upper rooms of Borley Rectory, and there are rooms in
other houses in which I would not sleep. But there actual
experience ends. For the rest, this book is a collection of
tales told and tales collected, many at first hand and others
from sources as sound as any from which a ghost may spring.
If it sends you to bed with no worse than a delicious shiver
and provokes no more ill than the memory of a forgotten
legend told as childhood truth, it will have served its enter-
taining purpose.

J. WENTWORTH DAY.

CHAPTER I

The Strangling Ghost

THE house sits, like a very old lady sunning herself, amid lilies and lavender within a rampart of yew hedges set in a flat green park, laced with shining brooks, against a tapestry of ancient woods. It is an old house. For it was built in the first half of the fifteenth century, in the reign of Henry VI, when the feudal power of the barons had neared its convulsive climax. The oaken timbers of its skeleton were driven into the earth half a century before Columbus sailed to discover America. They were cut from the forest oaks that surround the house, oaks which were seedlings, like enough, when William Rufus hunted the tall deer through its parkland glades.

An astute courtier of Henry VI began to build this ancient house within its forest manor in 1442 and finished it in 1466. He put in the magnificent display of nineteen tall windows of heraldic glass, probably the finest domestic glass of its kind

5

in the country. After the courtier's family came another, and then, in 1587, my ancestor, Doctor William Day, twelfth Provost of Eton, Dean of Windsor, and later Bishop of Winchester, bought it. The first Elizabeth had Bishop Day in mind for the Archbishopric of Canterbury, but he died too soon. His son, William, who lived on in the old house, married Helen Wentworth, daughter of Paul Wentworth, M.P., of Burnham Abbey, Bucks., son of Sir Nicholas Wentworth, Chief Porter of Calais and one of the great Wentworth family which held several hundred manors in Yorkshire, Essex, Suffolk, Buckinghamshire, and Berkshire.

The Days remained in their oaken house until 1801 or thereabouts, 214 years of continuous family history in one of the loveliest examples of a fifteenth-century manor-house left in England.

Then, by a fantastic turn of fortune, the old house, which had fallen on evil days, a place of rats and bats, of dust and dim cobwebs, was bought some fifty years ago by a baronet who was a notable antiquarian, a great connoisseur of fine armour and old furniture, and a good sportsman. His wife was a descendant of the Plantagenet courtier who built this "Oaken Place" more than five hundred years ago. Thus, in fantastic fashion, the old house came back to descendants of its creator.

Now this old house, which has all the ancient bloom of a missal, is no great mansion. It is an old manor-house of a very ancient and comfortable sort, the house-place of a knight or squire. Its windows are diamond-paned and mullioned; its walls of herring-bone brick and hewn oak are flushed with the warmth of forgotten summers. The colour ebbs and flows on the four great peaked eaves of the roof like lights on water: now old rose, then plum-purple, shading into amber, a delicacy of merged and flowing colours, with the wink of glass and the blush of old brick.

And when you go in at the front door, huge and dark grey, heavily studded with nails and banded from side to side by great iron hinges, you step into the Great Hall, forty-one feet long and thirty-six feet high from floor to roof-tree. The walls are hung with the torn banners of forgotten battles, the bright tapestries of vanished bowers. The light filters through high windows blazoned with the coats of arms of Plantagenet kings, knights, and barons. Two knights in full fighting armour and a man-at-arms in chain-mail gleam like silver ghosts in the rich dusk. The wide hearth, above which rises a great stone chimney-piece in which are still faintly nicked the initials of Yorkist men-at-arms who slept huddled on the floor when the Wars of the Roses swept the land, is creamy with the ashes of a wood fire that smoulders, year in, year out. The whole house, when one entered, was scented with wood-smoke.

If you step out of the Great Hall, silvery with the gleam of sword and lance, gorget and helm, horse-armour and demi-suits, its panelled walls golden in the rich half-light from those tall and coloured windows, you walk, beneath the carved screens, into a broad corridor that encloses the little inner courtyard round which the house is built. There is a guard-room on the left where men, armed and alert, did their daily sentry-go when the sixth Henry was on the throne.

Above the guard-room is the Henry VI Room, in which, they say, the monarch slept, for the builder of this house was a courtier high in royal favour. It is, like the other bed-rooms, oak-panelled from floor to ceiling, a high room, spanned from side to side, far up, by a great beam which springs from wall to wall. And in this room stands a four-poster bed, huge and oaken, carved with the arms of Catherine of Aragon. The furniture is all of a piece, as indeed is most of the furnishing in that ancient house.

So that if you went to bed in the Henry VI Room or, for that matter, in the Queen Elizabeth Room, in which that peripatetic monarch did actually sleep, you clambered into a vast open bed beneath a carved canopy resplendent with

Tudor roses and lozenges, with hangings that drew to on either side, until you were, in fact and feeling, enclosed in a little room within a room. On the floor, in the days when I dwelt there, were rush mats of the sort that the Tudors knew. By the bedside was an oaken manchet, a little cupboard in which, four centuries ago, they kept a thumb-piece of bread and cheese and a little flagon of wine lest a guest should wake hungry in the night. When you lived or stayed in that house you lived with the living past.

Do you wonder that when I first came to it in the rich glow of a winter sunset that lit the old trees in the park with flames of red-gold and turned the woods steel-blue and saw the face of this old house, dreaming in the last level rays under a sky of apple-green and amber, its windows winking with a thousand points of light, that I felt a sense of being watched? There stood the house, secret and only half seen, a chimney slim against the sky, the great eaves cocked like sun-bonnets, a mullioned window winking like a diamond, the old strange smell of wood-smoke, acrid in the dusk. A cat-owl mewed from an arrow-slit in the curtain-wall. And a brown owl answered him from a stag-headed oak out in the park, where wild duck quacked and spattered in the running brook.

And the house stood there, dark and quietly warm, watching one. There were windows that showed no lights, whose little diamond panes winked back no welcome from the last watery beam of the winter sun. They held secrets, very old and family things. There were faces, half guessed behind those upper windows of empty chambers, faces of young girls, pale and gone and long-forgotten, like flowers whose scent lingers ghostly; faces of young men killed in wars whose clangour is long stilled, and of grave men and old women, once wise and now dust, all of them part of the life and structure of this old house which was their home.

And as one stepped through the great oaken porch, under the screens and into that Great Hall with the sharp scent of half-burned logs, the haunting smell of wood polished and of wood burned, of old tapestries full of dust and of polished armour, there came again the sense, acute and overpowering, of watching eyes—eyes that looked down from the high gallery where once the minstrels played and the serving-maids peeped shyly upon the great ones at meat below.

There is often this sense of bygone presence, of watching eyes, usually very kindly and merely curious eyes, in old houses. The impress of their personalities is left strongly. It is a something inexpressible, ineluctable, undefinable, yet it is there. The merely material are insensitive to it. Some, perhaps, feel it, but since their canons are orthodox, they deny it. Nevertheless, it is a place of very old memories, and, I would say, of gentle ghosts.

That, however, has not been the experience of at least two people who have stayed there. Mr. Ernest Thesiger, the distinguished actor and a member of the gifted family which produced both a Lord High Chancellor and a Viceroy of India within living memory, apparently spent an unhappy night in the house.

In his book of memoirs, *Practically True,* he says:

Wherever we went we were put up by the kind inhabitants of the town in which we were to perform, and once the company passed an interesting but miserable night at the beautiful fourteenth-century place, —— Manor, which is the most un-doubtedly haunted house I have ever slept—or attempted to sleep —in. The door of my room had a heavy iron latch which I care-fully closed, but no sooner was I in bed than I heard a "clip-clop" of the latch, and the door swung slowly open. I got out of bed and examined the latch—lock there was none—and once more shut the door, taking special care to see that the latch was securely fastened. But the moment I had put out the light I heard the same "clip-clop", and the door again opened. This time I was far too much alarmed to get out of bed, and, burying my head under the bed-clothes, attempted to sleep. Luckily my room was the dressing-room of a larger room, which was occupied by my

cousin, Stephen Powys, an excellent amateur with whom I frequently acted, and I found to my relief that he was as nervous as
I was, so we kept the communicating-door between our rooms
open all night, to our mutual comfort.

The next morning we found that everyone else in the house,
with the exception of the hostess, who was presumably hardened
to ghosts, had been kept awake by mysterious sounds. One girl
told me that the occupant of the room next to hers had been
sobbing all night, but when we made inquiries we learnt that the
room in question was unoccupied. . . .

That, however, was mild compared with the experience of
the man who came to stay as my guest while my wife and I
were living there for some months, in 1942, as guests of the
then owner.

Now, since this is a ghost tale, let us consider the character
of the man who said that he suffered the greatest fright of
his life from a ghost within that house. He is now dead, but
I am afraid I can say little that is good about him. Since I
had business to do with him, it was necessary to invite him
for a week-end. I warned my host that my visitor was no
very pleasant personality. His wise old eyes looked at me
with a queer, sardonic twinkle.

"Ah, well," he remarked, "as you say that he hates all old
things, I think we'll put him to sleep in the Henry VI
Room." I wondered slightly at the reason for his quiet
chuckle, since I had not heard all the legends of the house.

My guest arrived late one evening with a brand-new
double gun-case and a fat and fluffy golden retriever, and
clad in a shooting suit of effulgent checks. His startled gaze
took in armour and bannerets, wood ash and rush mats,
candle-gloom and the figure of my host, in one sweeping
glance of incredulous scorn.

After dinner, at which he expounded his wealth, expanded
on his motor-cars and extolled his prowess at tame pheasants,
he and I retired to a little panelled parlour, where we settled
our business. Then, in a reek of Egyptian cigarettes, he

remarked with infinite condescension: "Well, you may like this queer old place, but give me central heating, concealed lighting, and a damn good bar!" And upon this note he retired to bed.

Night and the cry of owls descended upon the old house. The lights went out. At some time in the small hours I heard, from the Henry VI Room, a crash and a heavy thud. The lights went on in my guest's windows. They stayed on. At breakfast there descended a pale and slightly hollow-eyed magnate with a gun-metal complexion and an air of uneasy resentment. He announced brusquely that he was leaving immediately.

"But I hoped that we were going to offer you a day's shooting," my host remarked gently. "We've still got a fair stock of wild pheasants, in spite of too many foxes and carrion crows."

"No, thank you," my guest snapped. "I've got a big day on in Hampshire. They rear 'em by the cartload there. It's a real shoot." A little unkind, I thought.

I saw him off at the front door after our host had wished him well and wandered off to his library. There my guest rounded on me savagely.

"What d'you mean, asking me to stay in this rat-ridden old ruin?" he snapped. "Never again! Do you know, something tried to throttle me last night! I'd barely got to sleep when some fellow got me by the throat and tried to strangle me. I hit out, smashed the water bottle to bits, and knocked that old wooden bread cupboard, that—manchet, did you call it?—over. There wasn't a soul in the room, but I could hardly get my breath. I switched the lights on and left 'em on. The damn place is haunted. It's not fit for a civilised man to live in. I'm off!"

"A queer fellow, your guest," my host remarked, when I joined him a few minutes later. "Not at all nice mannered. I'm glad you warned me about him. He looked as if he hadn't slept very well."

"He didn't," I replied. "He said that something or somebody tried to strangle him during the night."

"Ah! They would!" he remarked, with that quietly sardonic smile which I had seen earlier. "You see, the Henry Room was the Justice Room in the old days. They used to hang the bad evil-doers from that great beam! It still seems to work, though it's many years since anyone felt it. I once had a fellow staying here, a charming person who had married a really wicked woman. They slept in that room for a week without any trouble. But when he had to spend one night in London and she was left here alone, she woke up just after midnight, screaming her head off, and rushed into my wife's room saying that someone had tried to strangle her! She left that day. We weren't sorry. We liked her husband—and I often wondered if the fright did do her any lasting good. It might even improve your peculiar friend—but I doubt it!"

A week later a very old lady from the village, nearly ninety years of age, came up to the manor-house. She sat in the Great Hall with me and ran over her memories of the far-off days when her mother was serving-maid to the farmers who followed my ancestors in possession of the place.

"They stored the potatoes and the sacks of corn in this Great Hall, sir," she lamented, "and the rats ran about as big as puppy dogs. Half the rooms were empty, but that room up there"—she pointed up to the Henry VI Chamber—"was always kept boarded up. We children were told not to dare go near it. There was something in there that would throttle yer!

"They did say that in the old days it was always called the Dungeon, because they used to hang the bad people in there. This house, being built on the flat so close to the water, they couldn't dig down and make a dungeon, so they hung 'em upstairs. We children peeked through the chinks in the boards many a time and we allus reckoned there was some great big black old thing in there with starey eyes—

The Justice Room

but, lor! I wouldn't go in that room then or now, not for a pension."

Thus the memory of the medieval Justice Room lingered on in village legend, as indeed it does to this day.

Three days after the midnight "visitation" in the Henry VI Chamber, I spent a couple of nights away from the house, shooting. My wife was left alone with our aged host; his companion-housekeeper, an educated woman; her soldier son, home on leave from the army, and Sparke, the butler, a matter-of-fact fellow about whose ears a dozen goblins might have buzzed with impunity. Creaks and squeaks never bothered him. Soon after dinner on the first night after my departure a chill draught blew through the Great Hall, and the door of the library in which the four of them were sitting blew open. It opened on to the glazed cloisters or corridor which encircle the inner courtyard.

The figure of a man, grey and distinct, passed the door in the corridor. Thinking it was the butler, the housekeeper called out: "Sparke!"

There was no reply. She walked to the door and looked along the corridor. The figure was just turning the corner. She called again. There was no answer. Her son ran after the figure. When he reached the corner of the corridor it had vanished.

Then he went in the kitchen. Sparke, the butler, was sitting there, smoking his pipe, reading the evening paper. He said that he had not moved since dinner was cleared.

Thoroughly alarmed now, the two women, the butler, and the soldier son toured the house armed with a shotgun, a revolver, and the fire-irons. They did not tell our host, who was dozing by the library fire. Not a thing nor a soul did they find. Nothing had been stolen. The only odd fact was that the great outer door, which Sparke swore that he had locked and barred as usual, was unlocked, its massive iron bars hanging inert from their staples.

Then they rang up the police. Police arrived, searched the house and found nothing. Not even a footprint. Yet two grown-up people swear to this day that they saw the very solid figure of a grey man walk down the corridor and vanish. Sparke stuck to it that he barred and bolted the outer door, the only way in. What do you make of that? The odd thing is that the grey figure had never been seen before or since.

As for my flamboyant friend, the victim of the Strangling Ghost, it is a curious fact that although an exceptionally strong man in early middle age, he died raving mad within a year or so, clutching at his throat and "seeing things". This unhappy demise may have been due not so much to the attention of the Strangler as to the fact that he drank his way relentlessly through a case or more of whisky in the course of a long week-end.

Now, in justice to the house, let me say that, although I have sat up in the Great Hall many a time until well after midnight and walked the cloisters and the creaking corridors upstairs in the small hours, I have never seen there a ghost or the suspicion of one. There was always, as I have said, the sense that one was being watched by the friendly eyes of those long dead; the sense, too, of a warm companionship, an ancestral friendliness from past ages. But that is an atmosphere one finds in many old houses, particularly those where long family roots have continued. It is part of the spiritual atmosphere of the house, some part of the colour and continuity of a man's own background.

But one odd and quite inexplicable set of circumstances did happen to me personally. There was a little room called the Spanish Parlour, a room full of early pieces of furniture with a luminous picture, a Luini, on the wall, and a view through diamond-paned windows into the garden of yews and lilies and beyond them, to the flat park where cattle moved in stately peace and the woods stood, winter-blue, in the far distance.

That room was panelled in those days from floor to ceiling in ancient crimson leather stamped with gold. It was very rare and valuable, that leather of blood and gold which had come four centuries ago, they said, from the house of the Spanish Governor of Mexico City in the days when Spain held nearly all Central America in the bloody thrall of persecution and torture.

Now you would have said that to work in such a room with the sunlight striking through the windows and the pheasants crowing in the park and no sound anywhere in the old house but the slow ticking of a clock, the grunt of a dog dreaming in front of the fire, that here was the ideal place in which to write a book. And on that task I was engaged one day in the Spanish Parlour with my private secretary, an old family friend of many years standing. We had never, I think, had a cross word in twenty years.

But on this day of which I speak, no sooner had we settled down to work in the Spanish Parlour than my ideas dried up, the typewriter jammed up, and our tempers flared up.

I found it quite impossible to concentrate on anything. The typewriter, dumb, but mechanically perfect, almost seized up. My secretary exclaimed pettishly: "I can't work in this room. I *won't* work in this room! It's nearly driving me mad—why, I really do believe that if it was on a top floor I should feel like jumping out of the window! Let's get out of it."

We got out. We removed to another room, a barer room with no fire, no lovely Luini to beguile the eye, no connoisseur's pieces on which to sit, and instead of a view over the park, a vision of the hen-run.

But the ideas flowed. The typewriter started like a two-year-old. The secretarial temper dissolved into a seraphic smile—and work flowed easily, phrase and sentence no longer slipped from the grasp.

Now, how do you account for that? Later that day, I was told that no one could ever sit for any time, with ease, in the

Spanish Parlour. It was seldom or never used, although it was one of the better rooms on the ground floor with an enchanting view. But always there was the sense of oppression, of frustration, of acute mental agony. And, be it noted, that overmastering sense had never been known in the room until the walls were covered with the blazonry of Spanish leather, blood-red and gold, from the cruel and bloody days of Spanish magnificence and torture in Mexico City when Philip of Spain and the Inquisition were at the peak of their devilish power.

This I know, that if ever by a heaven-sent chance that ancient family home was to return to me, I would sleep without fear in the chamber of Henry VI, as I have slept many a night in Queen Elizabeth's room where the boards creak and the great latched door opens sometimes of its own accord with a ghostly "whee-ee", but there should be no Spanish leather on the walls and the Spanish Parlour would take a new name and return to its Plantagenet simplicity of oaken walls.

CHAPTER II

Talk of Ghosts

WE sat round the fire by candlelight. Outside the wind roared in the bare trees, and pale stars winked remotely. Within, we had no wireless, no electric light or gas, no telephone, and no central heating—merely the leaping flames of a wood and peat fire in a fireplace twelve feet wide and five feet high.

A fire which flickered on the oaken beams and paved floor of that five-hundred-year-old house which is my old home, set on a bleak ridge above the frozen, flooded Fens. Outside, the wild geese bayed like hounds beneath the stars. Shock-headed trees played a wind-song above the thatched roof. And, at the back of the ancient pastures, full of owl-haunted hollow trees, lay the brown and reedy wilderness of Wicken Fen, where the bittern booms on nights of spring.

And on such a winter night, the wind howling, the flood waters out on all the shining fens, and wild geese clanging in the night, we talked of ghosts.

It was a fit time and place while chestnuts were roasted and hot punch went round. Outside the wind roared in the bare trees. Pale stars winked remotely at a white and silent world. And since it was Christmas, we talked of ghostly thrills and enchantments, as English people have told at Christmas since time began. And from that talk this book began.

Now I doubt if the modern Londoner can talk with ease or pleasure of ghosts when he sits in a minute room in a centrally-heated flat, gazing into a two-bar electric fire and listening to the simian ineptitudes of a "white nigger" crooner, drowning his Cockney accent in the East Side gibberish of New York.

But in old houses, in halls and farms, and inns that sit by black woods, and cottages which lurk in lanes, ghosts are still in season from Christmas until the graves open on Twelfth Night and swallow the walking dead.

You see, we believe in ghosts in East Anglia—or, if we do not admit that we believe in them, we have a hair-raising collection of them. And why not? Is it not the old land of Thor and Odin, of Freya and St. Guthlac, of Fenris the Wolf and St. Ingulph—of old gods and old saints of Saxon and Dane, a land of once-wild fens and steaming meres, of bare and windy heaths and dark woods that run down to the lonely, shining sea? Those old fens were a very lurking place of demons and swart devils, of Wills-o'-the-Wisp and Black Dogs. And still today there is a North Sea magic in the night wind, the whisper of witch-wings under the stars.

It was on just such a winter night of wind in bare branches that I set out to walk from Upware, that lonely hamlet on the banks of the Cam, by way of Spinney Bank, which runs between the sighing reeds and brown waters of Wicken Fen and the peewit-haunted cattle marshes of Spinney Abbey. I had a gun and a dog. I have walked that bank a thousand times in the last forty years, in red winter dawns and on misty fen nights.

We had been shooting snipe and duck all day on the wild undrained levels of Adventurers' Fen. The moon was just coming up, red and round. It is the last place in all England where the swamps and reed-beds, pools and shining waterways of "the old Fen" are still much as they were when Hereward, the last of the Saxons, threw back the armies of the Conqueror and burned them and their boats in the reeds on Aldreth Causeway. And in the inn which sits on the river bank beneath great willows, I said casually: "Well, who's coming home by the bank?"

Not a man of that rough crew of turf-diggers, sedge-cutters, and dyke-dydlers who sat by the turf fire in the sanded, red-curtained parlour of the "Five Miles from Anywhere—No Hurry", would take the short cut by the bank that would have saved a mile on the road home.

"That owd Black Dog run there o' nights, master," said Jake Barton, spitting into the white ash of the turf fire. "Do[1] ye goo, he'll hev ye as sure as harvest. I 'ouldn't walk that owd bank, not if I had to goo to Hanover."[2]

"Ne me yet nayther," chimed in two or three. "Yew recollect what happened to one young woman. She up and died arter that owd Dog runned her!"

"Well, I'm going," says I. "Are you coming, Fred? Your way lies my way, and it'll save you half a mile."

Fred shied like a horse.

"No, sir! No, sir! Yew 'on't ketch me on that there bank not tonight ne yit any other night. I 'ouldn't goo theer not for the King o' England! Ah! Yew may hev that gret owd gun but if we'd got machine guns an' tin hats, I 'ouldn't goo. An' ef yew goo, the owd Dog'll hev ye, sure as harvest."

Fred spoke with finality. I have known him since we were both boys. He was my constant companion on days in the Fen. He could walk the ordinary man off his legs, jump a dyke like a greyhound, drink a quart, fight anyone. But he was scared—and admitted it.

[1] "Do" is East Anglian for "if".
[2] "Go to Hanover" in the Fens expresses attempting the impossible. It is a throwback to early Georgian days when the House of Hanover came to the throne.

Now a word about Spinney, its history and ghosts, of which the Black Dog is not least. Until 1952 my friend, Robert Fuller, that excellent and wise farmer, lived at Spinney and owned its land, but in the last century its tenant was one Golding, a gentleman-farmer. He rented the house and lands from my cousin, Miss Mary Hatch. Golding was an eccentric and a daredevil. He once drove a horse up the oaken stairs at Spinney to the first-floor landing, and then tried to get it down again. A collection of hard-riding farmers had betted him that the feat was impossible.

It seemed so. Golding stamped, swore, and cracked his whip. The horse neighed, snorted, and kicked the banisters to blazes. Finally it reared and charged headlong down the stairs, slipped at the bottom, skidded among the scared guests, scattering them like chickens, and bolted straight out of the open front door. The hoof-marks can still be seen on the stairs.

Spinney has several ghosts. No place is better fitted for them. Founded by Lady Mary Bassingbourne, "of the Wykes", in the twelfth or thirteenth century, it was a lonely outpost of the Augustinian Canons, standing grey and grim, enisled amid reedy leagues of fen and mere. A bare wind-twisted belt of scrubby firs was all that protected it from the wild nor'-easters that howled down on the wings of the frost and battered its doors, rattled its windows, and beat flat the winter reeds in the great fish-stews.

They lived a good life, those old monks—asceticism offset by old wine and the best that the Fen netsmen and decoy-men could bring as tribute. It was too good to last. When Henry VIII fell upon them Spinney suffered with the rest. That is how the first ghosts began their earthly span.

The legend is that when Henry's men-at-arms marched on Spinney, the monks fled in terror down the subterranean passage which is supposed to connect the Abbey with Denny Abbey, five miles across the fens, on the other side of the Cam. They took with them the plate and all else moveable of value. Half-way down the tunnel they met the monks of Denny, who also had been turned out by Henry's ruffians.

They decided that it were better to yield up the holy treasures and be saved than perish and be glorified. So they trotted back to Spinney. There they found the Abbey wrecked and cast down, and tons of debris over the door to the outer world. The same had happened at Denny.

Thus the monks expiated their carnal backslidings by dying in that nightmare tunnel. Some of my family tried to explore the tunnel fifty years or more ago, but it was full of water and noisome gases.

In 1941, when I set out on horseback to ride a thousand miles through East Anglia, I came across two sets of singing ghosts. The first was at Spinney Abbey where, said Robert Fuller, "One morning at breakfast on Low Sunday, a few years ago, we heard ghostly singing out in the stack-yard, fourteen feet above the ground. It was clear as a bell. In fact, I thought at first it was the wireless. But no—there it was, pure and sweet, all in Latin, a dozen feet up in the air— just where the old Chapel of the Abbey used to stand. What do you make of that?"

I made as much—or as little—as I did of it when, a week later, at that sweet, bright old house in Thetford called The Canons, my host, Dr. Jameson, pointing out of the window to the gaunt, silvery grey ruins of the great Chapel of the Priory of the Holy Sepulchre, at whose foot lies buried all that is left of the once-mighty Hugh Bigod, said:

"One Sunday morning in May 1937, we heard distinct singing in Latin in that roofless chapel, a whole choir singing for half an hour. Then the sound of a man's feet walking slowly up the stone aisle—it's all grass now, anyway—and a man's voice reading prayers in Latin. It was so clear that I almost heard every word. How do you account for that?"

Apart from singing, the monks of Spinney seem to have contented themselves with tapping at midnight on the under-side of the bricked-over entrance to the tunnel, which is in the cellars—the only remaining portion of the original building. Robert Fuller told me some years ago that the banging was so loud one night that neither he nor his wife could sleep. At other times footsteps have been heard and horrible sliding, serpentine rustles, as of gigantic snakes slipping about on the brick steps.

Water fills the tunnel to within a few steps of the top. It is extremely probable that the river has broken in at some time and flooded the passage. This belief has given rise to stories that the tunnel is inhabited by great eels, which accounts possibly for the "slippery ghosts".

Whether there are eels or not is more than I can say, and the length of the tunnel is a moot point, for although there is undeniably a similar entrance at Denny, to a presumably similar tunnel, it seems inconceivable that the rude engineers of the Middle Ages should have been able to bore for five miles beneath a quaking bog of mud and water, with the bed of the Cam as an additional obstacle. It is hard to see, moreover, why two such obscure and unimportant monastic cells —neither was truly an abbey—should have been of such importance as to warrant so great an expenditure of money and labour.

Against this, however, must be set the fact that workmen who were "dydling out" a dyke on the fens about a mile from Spinney some thirty or more years ago, found the arched brick roof of a tunnel which seemed to run in a straight line between the two abbeys. The men got down to gault before they struck the roof, so it is just possible that the tunnel might have been driven through the sticky tenacious gault with little fear of inundation from the marshes above. Gault is impervious to water. But to hie back to our ghostly Dog.

"What are you scared of, Fred? Do you think you'll find a dead monk in the ditch?" I asked.

"No, I ain't skeered of no monkses. That's the Dog. He run along that bank o' nights, big as a calf, Master Wentworth, black as night, wi' eyes that glower at you like bike lamps! Do he see you you'll up and die. There ain't a man living what can see that owd Dog and live. Do he does, he'll goo scatty."

"But my father went along this bank scores of nights after duck, Fred. He said the best place for flight was by the old black mill."

"Dessay he did, but he niver seed the Dog. Do he'd ha' been a dead 'un."

Then Fred told me that only a few years previously his sister, on her way to meet her sweetheart at a moonlight tryst by the black draining mill, had seen it.

"Big as a calf, sir, he cum along that bank quiet as death. Jest padded along head down, gret old ears flappin'. That worn't more'n twenty yards off when that raised that's head and glouted [glared] at her—eyes red as blood. My heart! She did holler. She let out a shrik like an owd owl and belted along that there bank like a hare. Run, sir! There worn't nuthin' could ha' ketched her. I reckon if we'd ha' sent her to Newmarket she'd ha' won the Town Plate for us! She come bustin' along that bank like a racehoss, right slap into her young man. Ha! She did holler. And then, when he collared hold of her, she went off dead in a faint!"

"Did her young man see anything, Fred?"

"Nit nothin'!"

"Well, she's still alive, isn't she, Fred? The Dog didn't kill her, after all."

"Ha! Take more'n an owd Dog to kill her. She's as tough as hog leather. But that wholly laid her up for a week and she've bin a'clan-janderin' about it ever since."

So Fred did not walk with me by Spinney Bank that night. The presence of a double eight-bore and the promise of a quart of beer failed to shake the prestige of the Dog. And when I told him next day that I had walked home alone that night by the bank he answered: "More fule yew! But then, happen the owd Dog don't hut the gentry!"

This legend of a ghostly dog persists all over East Anglia.

A very dear friend, a Norfolk peeress of the old school, one about whom there was "no nonsense, my dear" believed in it implicitly. She had seen it!

One night at Leiston in Suffolk, on the coast, where the Dog is known as "The Galleytrot", she and the then Lady Rendlesham sat up in the churchyard to watch. At twelve precisely a slinking, sable shadow slipped among the gravestones like a wraith, leaped the low churchyard wall and slid down the dark lane towards the sandhills like an evil whisper. Neither of those self-possessed ladies drank, sat up late or had ever heard of Hannen Swaffer.

Now this Black Dog of the Fenland is the same mythological animal as Black Shuck, the enormous ghostly hound of the Norfolk coast who is said to pad along the cliff-top path between Cromer and Sheringham.

On the high coast road that goes dipping down through woods and over heathy commons where the sea-wind blows, between Cromer and Sheringham, there are villages whose inhabitants will not walk the windy miles of that lonely road at night if you were to offer them ten pounds and a cask of beer.

They are scared, these hardbitten Norfolk fishermen and ploughmen.

W. A. Dutt, in his book, *The Norfolk Broadland,* says:

> One of the most impressive phantoms, and one of the best known in Norfolk, is Old Shuck (from the Anglo-Saxon, Scucca or Sceocca, the early native word for Satan), a demon dog, as big as a fair-sized calf, that pads along noiselessly under the shadow of the hedgerows, tracking the steps of lonely wayfarers, and terrifying them with the wicked glare of his yellow eyes. To meet him means death within the year to the unhappy beholder. As Shuck sometimes leaves his head at home, though his eyes are always seen as big as saucers, he is, as Mr. Rye says, "an animal more avoided than respected". One of his chief haunts is Neatishead Lane, near Barton Broad; but he also favours Coltishall Bridge, over which he always ambles without his head; and

a very special promenade of his is from Beeston, near Sheringham, to Overstrand, after which his course is uncertain. Which recalls the old adjuration in the legend of St. Margaret:

> Still be thou still,
> Poorest of all, stern one,
> Nor shalt thou, Old Shock,
> Moot with me no more.
> But fly, sorrowful thing,
> Out of mine eyesight,
> And dive thither where thou man
> May damage no more.

Mr. Dutt has more to say on the topic in his *Highways and Byways in East Anglia*:

It is not the children only who go about at night in fear of Black Shuck. If this were a stormy night instead of a stormy day, the old fisher-folk of the coast would say it was just the time for Black Shuck to be abroad; for he revels in the roaring of the waves and loves to raise his awful voice above the howling of the gale. Black Shuck is the "Moddey Dhoo" of the Norfolk coast.

He takes the form of a huge black dog and prowls along dark lanes and lonesome field-paths, where, although his howling makes the hearer's blood run cold, his footfalls make no sound. You may know him at once, should you see him, by his fiery eye; he has but one, and that, like the Cyclops, is in the middle of his head. But such an encounter might bring you the worst of luck; it is even said that to meet him is to be warned that your death will occur before the end of the year. So you will do well to shut your eyes if you hear him howling—shut them even if you are uncertain whether it is the dog-fiend or the voice of the wind you hear.

Should you never set eyes on our Norfolk Snarleyow, you may perhaps doubt his existence, and, like other learned folks, tell us that his story is nothing but the old Scandinavian myth of the black hound of Odin, brought to us by the Vikings who long ago settled down on the Norfolk coast. Scoffers at Black Shuck there have been in plenty; but now and again one of them has come home late on a dark, stormy night, with terror written large on his ashen face and after that night he has scoffed no more.

A curious variation of this ghostly hound is said to haunt an overgrown and little-used lane called Slough Hill in the parish of West Wratting on the Suffolk borders of Cambridgeshire. Police Constable A. Taylor, of The Tiled House, Panton Street, Cambridge, tells me that, in his youth, this lane which is on the road from West Wratting to Balsham was haunted by an extraordinary thing called "the Shug Monkey". It was, he says, "a cross between a big rough-coated dog and a monkey with big shining eyes. Sometimes it would shuffle along on its hind legs and at other times it would whizz past on all fours. You can guess that we children gave the place a wide berth after dark!"

He adds that Spanneys Gate into West Wratting Park was haunted by a White Lady.

Another alive and kicking believer in the Black Dog is Mrs. Sophia Wilson, a native of Hempnall, near Norwich. Mrs. Wilson writes to me:

> There is a stretch of road from Hempnall called "Market Hole" and when I first lived at Hempnall sixty-one years ago, my husband told me that there was something to be seen and had been seen by different residents.
>
> Well, my dear husband passed on and I never really thought anything more about the incident until one night my son who was then about twenty-four came in from Norwich looking white and scared. I said, "Whatever is the matter? Are you ill?" and he said, "No. Coming down Market Hole I had a bad turn. I saw what appeared to be a big Dog about to cross in front of my bike and I thought I should be thrown off, but it just vanished. When I got off my bike and looked round, there was nothing to be seen, and I felt awful."
>
> I am afraid I have not put this together very well, but it's quite true and I hope you will include it in your book, which I shall be happy to read.

Another version of Black Shuck is said to haunt villages in the Waveney Valley round about Geldeston. It is known as "The Hateful Thing" or "The Churchyard or Hellbeast", and although usually seen in the form of a huge dog, it has been known to take the shape of a "Swooning Shadow", whatever that may be. It is a sign that some unusually horrible wickedness has just been committed or is about to be.

There seems little doubt that the Hateful Thing is no more than a garbled local version of Black Shuck. Morley Adams, who wrote that almost forgotten work, *In the Footsteps of Borrow and Fitzgerald,* quotes a story told more than half a century ago by an old village woman who claimed that she saw it when walking home at night from Gillingham to Geldeston. She tells the story in the following words:

> It was after I had been promised to Josh and before we were married that I saw the "Hateful Thing". It must have been close upon the time that we were to be married for I remember we had got as far as "waisting" it.
>
> It was between eight and nine and we were in a lane near Geldeston when we met Mrs. S. and she started to walk with us, when I heard something behind us, like the sound of a dog running. I thought that it was some farmer's dog, and paid little attention to it, but it kept on just at the back of us, pit-pat-pit-pat-pit-pat! "I wonder what that dog wants," I said to Mrs. S. "What dog do you mean?" said she, looking all round.
>
> "Why, can't you hear it?" I said, "it has been following us for the last five minutes or more! You can hear it, can't you, Josh?" I said. "Nonsense, old mawther," said Josh, "just you lug hold of my arm and come along." I was walking between Josh and Mrs. S. and I lay hold of Mrs. S.'s arm and she says, "I can hear it now; it's in front of us; look, there it be!" And sure enough just in front of us was what looked like a big, black dog; but it wasn't a dog at all; it was the "Hateful Thing" that had been seen hereabouts before and it betokened some great misfortune.
>
> It kept in front of us until it came to the churchyard, when it went right through the wall and we saw it no more.

29

She said that many people in the district had seen it and that its favourite haunt was the "Gelders" which was a local name for a clump of trees by the wayside on the Beccles Road. Morley Adams adds:

> I found from conversation with other folk in the neighbourhood that her words were quite true; but apart from this woman, I found no one who had actually seen the beast, but they all knew someone who had. I gained the following further information about this weird wraith: At times it is seen as a large black dog, with eyes of fire and foaming mouth. If no fear is shown, he will walk just behind you, but his paws make no sound upon the ground. The person who sees him should not attempt to turn back or the beast will growl and snarl like a mad dog. He has been known to drag children along the road by their clothes, and dire disaster overtakes the individual who persists in running away from him.
>
> The people who are most likely to see the "Hell-hound" are those born under the chime hours, or towards the small hours of a Friday night.

The same Dog runs in Essex along the lonely coast road from Peldon to Tolleshunt D'Arcy. William Fell, gamekeeper of D'Arcy, swears to me that he has seen it twice on Wigborough Hill.

The Black Dog is one with the Ghostly Hound of Dartmoor who haunts the moor and hunts terrified humans to their death in the quaking bogs. The Hound of the Baskervilles is a Dorsetshire version. All have their roots in the Hound of Odin, the mighty dog of war, whose legend came to Britain a thousand years ago when the long-ships grounded in the surf, the ravens flew at their mastheads, there was battle and the clang of swords in the swirling mists, and "all around the shouts of war and the cries of sea-raiders beaching their ships".

So the old myths endure. Even my Board-School-educated Fred and his cinema-going sister would not walk on Spinney Bank in the moon, between the wild fen and the cattle pastures. They would not walk there for all the gold in Fort Knox or all the land in Britain.

The countryman is seldom a scoffer at ghosts. He may tell you that it is all old women's stuff and that no one has ever seen a thing, but, deep in his heart, he cherishes the old legends. They were part of his childhood and of the childhood of his fathers and great-grandfathers, harking back to stories of the first Elizabeth's day or the misty pages of Saxon history. They are part of his background, and he does not let them slip into forgetfulness.

If you want a gentler sort of dog, there is, or was, that completely unknown ghost-hound, the Black Dog of Leeds Castle in Kent. None of that numerous band, the professional ghost retailers, know of his existence. He is, or was, a strictly family dog. His appearances usually portended some sort of disaster to the old owners of that lovely lake-castle, the Wykeham-Martins.

But the old owners departed after 1918, and Leeds today is a new castle. The old rooms have vanished and new have taken their place. Leeds, which once was old and comfortable, Victorian and stuffy, is now mock-medieval, furnished according to Fortnum, and quite too terribly smart. It would look rather well in America.

So I sometimes wonder if the Black Dog is still there. He may not approve of mock-medievalism.

Have you ever seen Leeds, the "fairy castle of Kent", as the guide-books invariably lyricise it? It is grey and lovely, built on three islands in the heart of a lake. The lake lies in one of the oldest parks in Kent. The walls rise sheer from the lake, their towers and battlements, windows and machicolations mirrored in lily-dappled waters. There is a Great Tower and an outer bailey, a grey stone bridge across the moat, a green inner court where Normans and English tilted in the centuries when Leeds was young. There are dungeons and chill passages cut in the massive stone walls.

So do you wonder that Leeds has a ghost? Yet I wonder that its ghost should be so gentle a wraith. A Black Dog who walks gently across the room whilst one is at tea or, suddenly, without fuss, materialises on the hearth-rug, is no fit and apposite ghost for a castle where they discovered a skeleton curled up in the final agonies of death in a tiny torture cell only four feet square . . . a cell where the prisoner could neither sit, lie, nor stand. Yet in spite of the nightmare deaths and horrors unbelievable which Leeds must have witnessed in its history, the Dog alone remained as its sole supernatural heritage.

Those who have seen him, and I had this from Charlie Wykeham-Martin of the old family, say that he was a medium-sized animal, black, curly-haired and fairly large in the ear—obviously a retriever. All the tales of him are plain, homely tales, tales you would hear of any lovable dog in any house . . . with the slight difference that this Dog disappears into the wall, door, or window just as one is beginning to appreciate his finer points.

The old nurse had seen it one year and the young master had died . . . or, warned in time, the old nurse had run to the moat-edge just in time to gaff the young master from a fishy grave. Another year the under-housemaid had seen the Dog, sleeping in a passage, trotting towards her or crossing a room and melting into the opposite wall . . . and the under-house-maid had promptly up and died or been jilted by her young man. Those were the sorts of tale. So you see that the Dog of Leeds was catholic in the significance of his appearances. It is as though he said: "I love you all too well to wish you harm but, as I must coincide with catastrophe, look out!"

That was what happened to the lady of the old family whom I know and who told me this true tale. She sat one autumn afternoon in a great mullioned bay-window which overhung the moat and gazed across the ancient park. That window, deep within, rose and grey without, had gazed out over the park for six centuries or more. It had seen the Saxon deer graze under the oaks, heard them roar to the winter skies and had known the clamour of men-at-arms setting out for war. Long generations of the old families who made the name of Leeds great in English history had sat in that window over the moat. One would think that such a memory-filled old window was the best place for an hour in the pale sunlight of an autumn afternoon.

The Dog chose that moment for his first and only appearance before the lady of that house. He came suddenly, a perfectly solid black body of strokeable dog, from the direction of the door and walked across the room. She gazed at him with mild wonder. So far as she could remember there were no large, black, likeable-looking dogs in the *ménage* at the moment. But then, in any properly regulated house in the country, you never know when a new dog is not going to bestow his introductory lick on you. Which is one reason why the country is so much pleasanter a place to dwell in.

She gazed, as I say, at the dog and was preparing to call him when, without fuss, he vanished into the opposite wall. That is a disturbing thing to happen. The lady rose and crossed the room and examined this peculiar wall which could swallow large black dogs alive.

And, even as she crossed the room, the whole of that rose and grey window-seat fell into the moat! The masonry of six centuries plunged into the water in a fountain of foam. But for the Dog she would have plunged with it and no woman can swim well with a ton of old bricks on top of her.

So, you see, the Black Dog of Leeds is a gentle beast with a proper appreciation of the worth of a charming woman.

They have a different sort of legend on the Norfolk coast where Black Shuck runs—that of the Shrieking Pits of Aylmerton. No one knows who dug the pits or when or why. They have lain for hundreds of years in a green field near the village. And in the village they tell you that on summer

33

nights when the moon is high, the wind comes fresh and salty off the North Sea and bean fields scent the night, a woman in white walks round the Pits, weeping and wringing her hands. No man knows her history.

The Pits may go back to Neolithic days, for underground dwellings and pits dug for flints wherewith to make stone axes and arrowheads are commoner in Norfolk than most counties. I prefer to think that the dead of a great battle in Saxon days or village victims of the Black Death were buried in the pits and that, for them, the frail wraith in white weeps beneath the moon.

We have a female ghost of a different sort in my Cambridgeshire village of Wicken. She is a headless queen, who, on a midsummer midnight, gallops in her coach, drawn by four headless horses, and driven by a headless coachman, over twenty county bridges.

The queen is Anne Boleyn, whose head fell after she married Henry VIII. Her Norfolk home was Blickling Hall, that unbelievably lovely Elizabethan mansion which Lord Lothian gave to the National Trust. She sets out from there and drives through all the parishes of Norfolk, Suffolk, and Cambridgeshire, where her father, Sir John, held lands.

In my bleak fenland parish the coach rolls noiselessly down Red Barn Lane at midnight, crosses the "washes" of the River Cam in the mist, majestically takes the air and voyages over the river—where once was a bridge and now no bridge is. That is the village story.

Breccles Hall, that lovely Jacobean house in Norfolk, where the late Edwin Montague, one-time Secretary of State for India, had his home, has another ghostly lady. She arrives at midnight in a coach and four, attended by footmen, powdered and curled. The coach steps are let down, and, if the Hall is empty, every window springs into instant light and the curious may see a ball in full swing with lords and ladies and the squires of the county in Georgian dress. But if you look in her eyes as she steps from her coach you are a dead man. Jim Mace, a poacher, died of her eyes in the early 1900's. The story was told in *The Times*.

The Hall was empty and it was Christmas. Snow lay deep and the pheasants had gone crowing up to roost long ago. The gamekeeper was old, deaf, and in bed. Down in the village, farm labourers growled, in broad Norfolk, deep into their pewter pots. The inn fire flickered and leaped. Two of the younger men got up.

"Jimma bor and me is a-gooin' tu hev a brace or tu o' them longtails for Christmas," announced one. "The wind's a-blowin' wonderful an' the owd keeper on't hear us if we du shute." Older men tried to dissuade them.

"Yu'll hev the Christmas cooch and fower on yu'," said one old man. "An' ef yu du look in that lady's eyes yu be a dead 'un, bor."

Off they went, laughing. It was then ten o'clock. By near midnight the two poachers, using the old trick of a hollow bamboo pole and a tin of smouldering sulphur-covered rags, had "smoked" a dozen fat pheasants off their perches. They carried a short-barrelled gun, but had not fired a shot. Finally, they came out in front of the Hall. The old mansion, empty and black-windowed, stood stately in the moonlight, its roofs white with snow, its twisted chimneys and eaves sharp against the winter stars. Down in the village the church clock boomed out the first stroke of midnight.

Jim Mace, laughing, slipped out of the bushes and ran across to the front door, trying to peer in at a window "tu see them owd ghosties".

The last stroke of the clock boomed on the icy night. Round the bend in the carriage-way swept a coach and four, lamps blazing, footmen at the back, coachmen on top, four fine horses prancing—as silent as death.

The windows of the Hall sprang into instant light. A footman leaped down, pulled down the carriage steps, swept open the door, and out stepped the loveliest lady that poor Jim Mace had ever seen in his life, powdered, jewelled, with hair piled high and satin dress flounced royally. She gazed at the poor, scared farm boy, flattened by fear against the Hall door—and the most dreadful scream that Breccles Hall has ever heard cut the snowy silence like a knife.

Jim's friend bolted. He roused half the village, but not a man would go near the place that night. Jim did not come home. Next morning the parson, the clerk, and half the village went fearfully up to the deserted Hall. In the snow lay the frozen body of Mace, his face twisted in agony, his eyes wide open in the most awful expression of fear that man could wish to see. On the snow was no sign of wheeltrack or footmark.

They took the body away, and when the Coroner saw the frozen look of fear in the dead man's eyes he ordered that they be photographed to see if any last imprint of the thing which had stopped his heart-beat by terror was left on the retina. But there was nothing.

East Anglia is rich in ghosts and legends of ghosts, in witches and talk of wise women. I have told elsewhere of the witches of Foulness Island and the devil who threw the man downstairs one dark night at lonely Devil's House on Wallasea Island. There are plenty today in those coastal marsh villages who, if you were to tell them that Devil's House is so-called because, in the early sixteenth century, it belonged to the family of Duval, would smile slyly and secretly. And tell you no more.

If you want a tale of a different sort, go inland to Woolpit by Bury St. Edmunds, the capital city of Suffolk. Bury is so self-contained with its great Georgian and Queen Anne town houses of the old squirearchy; its magnificent Angel Hotel, which once had the best cellar of port and French wines in East Anglia; its soaring Abbey; its wide streets, markets and murmur of life that I doubt if it has ever heard much of London. If it had it would not be impressed.

Woolpit is a different matter, for Woolpit is not of this world. Nor has it anything to do with wool. The truth is that one night a farmer looked out of his window under the moon and saw a great, gaunt animal come out of a hole in the ground. He thought it was a calf. But when it lifted its ghastly head and bared its fangs he saw that it was a wolf.

Now wolves demand guns, especially when they appear in Suffolk. So the farmer went downstairs for his gun. But the wolf had gone. And, horror upon horror, it left no footprints.

If you cannot believe that story you must at any rate have no doubt of the Green Children. They also came out of the Wolf Pit at Woolpit. William of Newbury tells the tale. They were boy and girl, green all over, and they lived on green food given them by the villagers. They came, they said, from a twilight land which accounted for their colour. But very soon they got down to roast beef, boiled bacon and Suffolk dumplings. The appalling result was that they became quite normal flesh colour.

The boy died, but the girl grew up and married a man at King's Lynn, the port upon the Wash where the houses have crow-stepped gables and look as though they had stepped straight out of Bruges. This is merely to remind you that in East Anglia we had once the richest wool and weaving trade in all England, so rich that the Flemings and the Huguenots came hither in hundreds.

I could tell you a lot more—about the Wailing Wood near Thetford; of the Ghostly Skater who flies over Hickling Broad on frozen nights, and about the bells of lost churches which ring beneath the waves off Dunwich, the drowned city whose ships sailed to fight the Armada.

There is no room and no time to tell one tithe of such tales, and not all are tellable. For example, it is said that the Black Arts have been revived in South Wales today by a well-known novelist whose education could have led him into more useful fields than this second-hand exploitation of the shoddy, sensual, discredited practices of a primitive and ignorant past. There are villages within a few miles of

Swansea, where dreadful tales are told of orgies practised at midnight, of cats sacrificed, of young women persuaded to take part in rites which would mean imprisonment for all concerned were they discovered. This erotic searching to revive a pagan religion is as despicable as the actions of the adolescent who tortures a cat in order to persuade himself that he is a matador in a bull-fight. It is unworthy of any notice except that of the police.

What is interesting is the belief in the marshland parts of Essex and, more particularly, in the Island of Sark, in the powers of the local witch or "wise man". In Essex there are many villages where the witch can still tell your fortune by the stars, cure warts by tying a horse-hair about them, concoct a potion to cure the rheumatism or chant a spell to make the cows give more milk. This is harmless enough. Half their practices have an entirely sensible root in homely medicines.

Sark, that unique little feudal state in the Channel Islands, is ruled under a Charter of Queen Elizabeth, by a woman, my old friend, Mrs. Sybil Hathaway. She has her own army, her own Parliament, her own laws, and prohibits divorce and motor-cars. The people of Sark believe in witches so mightily that every old cottage has a "witch step" built into the chimney. This is a flat projection, placed about a foot below the chimney top. It is there to afford rest for the witches when they fly abroad at night. For, after all, if a witch should sit on your chimney-pot the draught of warm air might persuade her to go farther down the chimney, which would be dreadful for the boiling pot, terrifying for the children and most upsetting for the grown-ups. But if the witch, on her night flights, discovers a stone slab let into the chimney's side, where she may sit comfortably, her eyes to the stars, her back warmed by the flue, she will never dream of undertaking a sooty journey to lower and possibly warmer regions.

If you have any doubt that there are witches on Sark, La

The Hand of Glory

Dame will tell you herself that it is only a year or two ago that one of her prize cows was taken ill. All the veterinary surgeons in the Channel Islands failed to cure her. But when the village cow-man suggested that a "wise man" of the Island should be consulted, the cow recovered. The "wise man" merely tied a length of wool about one of the cow's legs. He announced that it would be all right in the morning. It was. And it still is. I have seen the cow myself and I know this story to be true.

The North Country legends of witches were more terrible, more ghoulish. There is that dreadful story they still half-believe in, deep in the Yorkshire moors, in the lost farms and lonely cottages of the dales. That is the story of the "Hand of Glory" with its dread command:

"Fly bolt, fly bar, fly lock.
Open thy door to the Dead Man's Knock."

Late in the night at a lonely inn, or stranded farmhouse in the dales, when mists shut down like blankets in the hills, when the moon struggled through a wrack of clouds, when cattle stirred sleepily in the stockyard and the moors slept beneath the ghostly whistle of flighting curlew, the inn-keeper or farmer would be disturbed by a sudden rapping on his front door.

Poking his night-capped head out of the window there was the horrifying vision beneath, of a group of hooded figures, whose leader held in his right hand the shrunken, withered hand of a dead man, its witch-like fingers crooked about the stump of a ghastly flaring candle with which he rapped upon the door, whilst the dread command was incanted again and again.

The man in the night-cap knew well enough that the dead man's hand had been cut from the swinging corpse of a highwayman, creaking in the chains of a cross-road gibbet. He knew that the tallow had been mixed from the fat of a

41

newer corpse, of a dead tom-cat and a par-boiled owl. He knew, too, that the wick had been twisted from the lank hair of the corpse of another highwayman. He knew that this candle, its flickering light, its ghastly message, were compounded of the earthly symbols of evil crime and the supernatural—of men who carry death by day, and of birds and animals that are the disembodied spirits of evil ones by night.

No wonder they unbolted the door, threw open the till, the safe, and the cellar. Do you wonder that for centuries this barbaric symbol of fear held half the North in a thrall of superstition?

There is no one today who believes in the "Hand of Glory". But there are lots of fools and neurotic women who believe in a backstairs soothsayer, a Mayfair crystal gazer, a Hindu fortune-teller, and a gipsy on Epsom Downs. The "Hand of Glory" is a dead symbol, the Black Arts are proscribed by the police. Witches no longer ride on broomsticks, corpses clank no more in chains, no ghostly highwayman rides Hounslow Heath or Barnby Moor—but the spirit of foolish superstition is still alive, translated into sixpenny fortunes on Epsom Downs and séances in Mayfair.

I like better that legend of a Norman ghost which I told in *Coastal Adventure* and take leave to tell here again. It goes back to a night of harvest moon when I stood on a low hill above the crawling creeks of the Essex coast, with the fields falling away from my feet to the sea-marshes, partridges calling, and behind me, in a thicket of trees, a tiny church, where lay a dead man whose heart was plucked out by the Devil.

Now you may not believe this part of my story, but I am assured that it is true. I was told it by a little old lady with pink cheeks and white hair in coils, with tiny hands and a soft voice which spoke the English of Surtees.

She dresses, this pretty old lady, in black bombazine with puffed sleeves such as they wore in Edward VII's day, and she lives in Norman England—that is to say, in the tiny

42

village of Tolleshunt D'Arcy. Can you doubt a pretty little old lady like that!

Tolleshunt D'Arcy is a haunting name, but no more beautiful than Tolleshunt Knights, or Follifaunts; than Layer Marney or Layer de la Haye, Layer Breton or Manifold Wick, Salcott-cum-Virley, or even Bradwell-juxta-Mare, which are names of villages and manors, forgotten since time began, stranded in that lost, sea-musical countryside that lies on either side of the great Blackwater estuary. There are moated farms and gull-dappled fields, Crusaders in the churches and ghosts in the deep lanes.

It is a land which the Romans knew and the Danes raided, the Saxons lost and the Normans dwelt in. And when the Normans had settled there and made peace with the sword, its history stood still. It has slept ever since. None but the fishermen and the smugglers have coloured the tale of its quiet days.

But ghosts and witches still walk and little old ladies still believe in Norman wraiths and tell of the Devil walking the highroad? This is the tale she told me:

You see that thicket on the hill by the Wigborough Road, sir. There, many years ago, a man set out to build Barn Hall [and Barn Hall, I may tell you, was built in about 1500, which shows the deep roots of Essex legends]. This man had two speyed-bitches that walked beside him always. Reg'lar fond o' them, he was.

Now, as he was a-settin' up the beams for to build Barn Hall, the Devil come up the road.

"Hey, there, what are you a-doin'?" the Devil hollered.

"I'm buildin' Barn Hall," the man said. "Me an' my two speyed-bitches are a-buildin' it together."

"You won't build Barn Hall here," the Devil said. And he picked up a beam and hulled it a mile, so that it stuck up in the ground in Tolleshunt Knights parish. "That's where you'll build Barn Hall," the Devil said, "where that beam fall!"

"I won't! I'll build it here—me and my two speyed-bitches'll do it in spite of you," the man said, defiant.

43

Now, you see, sir [my little old lady put in], that man made a wrong piece of statement there. If he'd said: "God an' me and my two speyed-bitches will do it," he'd had confounded the Devil. But he left God out—a very wrong thing to do, and one that led him into ways of confusion and hell fire.

Well, sir, the man went on buildin', and every night the Devil come and hulled down what he'd set up.

So they had a great argument, and the man said: "I'll beat you in the end."

"No, you won't," said the Devil, "I'll beat *you*. Because in the end you'll be dead, and wherever they bury you I'll come and rend the heart out of you. That's my curse upon you. May it lie!"

Well, sir, the man died, and he give orders that he was to be buried in the Bushes Church, over at Knights, because he said the Devil dussent go in the church after him.

But the parson at the Bushes said he couldn't be buried in the church, but must lie just outside, agin the wall.

And there they buried him . . . and in the night the Devil came on his wings and plucked out his heart.

If you go to that little old church, sir, you'll see inside the poor body of the man what was turned to stone when the Devil rent him.

I went, and in the chancel by the altar I found a stone knight, visored and legless, Stephen de Pateshull, whom Edward the Confessor planted in this lonely parish of scattered farms. There was a gash in his stone side.

In the dusk, with the partridges calling, I leaned on a gate with the rector, an erudite man, and told him the old lady's tale.

"They all believe it," he said, "but it's nonsense—except that there is a man buried close to, but outside, the church wall, as close as the law will allow." Which is queer if you come to think of it.

And I thought of that other ghost which haunts Mersea Island and of the dead-and-gone old lady who first told me the tale of it. Her grandson tells it today. And if you want

44

to hear it, why then, when next you go to Mersea Island, that pleasant land of fishermen and yachtsmen off the Essex coast, arrest your wheels at the Peldon Rose. The Peldon Rose is that ancient inn which lies about six miles from Colchester on the Mersea road. It is so ancient, this rose-red inn on the salty edge of the sea-marshes, that they have listed it as an Ancient Monument, which is an honour for any old inn.

Baring-Gould knew the Peldon Rose and made it a centre of drama in those Victorian novels over which our Victorian grandmothers shuddered.

And in the Peldon Rose I found my lady who remembered Baring-Gould—"a tall, thin man, who walked along the marsh roads singing, and was forever writing books about us".

This lady was Mrs. Jane Pullen, landlady of the Peldon Rose, then eighty-one years old, as active as a ballet dancer, as upright as a ramrod, with hands and feet as tiny as those of a doll.

Mrs. Pullen believed in ghosts. She walked with the ghost of a Roman centurion down the road from the Barrow Hills, on Mersea Island, to the causeway, whose glittering tides curdle on either hand. Now the Barrow Hills are simply Danish barrows and Roman tumuli, for West Mersea was a Roman settlement when the Count of the Saxon Shore garrisoned the fort of Othona at Bradwell, across the water. So why should not a Roman ghost walk on Mersea at night?

"He came down off the Barrow Hills," said Mrs. Pullen. "The steady tramp of a man's feet, like it was a soldier marching, and he caught up with me and walked all the way down to the Strood.

"I could see no one, yet the feet were close beside me, as near as I could have touched him.

"I bopped down to look along the road in the moonlight, yet no one was there. Still the feet kept on.

45

"I walked down the road till I came on a man I knew. He was all a-tremble. He shook like a leaf.

" 'I can hear him,' he said, 'but where is he? I can't see anyone.'

" 'Keep all along of me,' I said to the man, 'and no harm will come to you. 'Tis only one of those old Romans come out of the Barrows to take his walk.'

"And we walked on, sir—with the footsteps close beside us, till we turned up a lane, and he went on."

"Weren't you frightened?" I asked this pretty old lady with the alert eyes.

"Why should I be?" she asked. "I put my trust in God, and when you do that, naught can harm you. Besides, those old Romans do you no harm.

"My grandson, that is up in London, camped last summer on the Ray Island, and in the middle of the night a ghost walked up to his tent across the marsh in the bright moon—footsteps, and no sign of a man, and all as bright as day.

"My grandson left his tent and ran home like a scared little boy."

No one had told Mrs. Pullen's grandson that Ray Island and all the saltings about it are full of mounds of Roman and Saxon origin—mounds of charcoal, clinkers of fused sand, Samian pottery, and the like.

It was in about the sixties that a man was "scuffling about" on the top of Barrow Hills when the top of the mound gave way and he fell a dozen or more feet into a cave of inky blackness. In the cave they found a Roman pavement, some say an altar, the burial place of a forgotten centurion who ruled the island when the eagles gleamed and swung across the stony, salty Strood into the isle of oysters and wild geese. So perhaps the centurion, tired of his musty tomb, does sometimes take a walk on nights of springtide moons.

Do you wonder that they say that the spirits of the old Crusaders in the Essex churches are still alive? Do you wonder that they believe that John, Lord Marney, rises from his stone escutcheoned tomb in Layer Marney Church, or that the D'Arcys, ruffled and armoured, steal across the moat on moonlight nights from their cold lodgings in D'Arcy Church to the panelled rooms and raftered kitchen of D'Arcy Hall.

This old land of the Danes, asleep by day, is alive and awake beneath the moon at night.

CHAPTER III

They Walk the Battlefields

THE guns in Flanders were dead. In that last month of the grey winter of 1918 an eerie stillness dwelt on the battlefields of France and Belgium. Dead lay unburied in fields and sodden trenches. Guns and rifles, shells and Mills bombs lay rusting. Warneton Ridge was a wilderness of mud and crawling wire, shell-pocked and lonely as the wind. Mont Kemmel, "The Gibraltar of Northern France", alone with its dead and its torn trees, loomed above the grey plains that have been Europe's cockpit for centuries.

By day carrion crows croaked deathlike from shattered trees, travesties of nature whose bare trunks were bullet-scarred and shell-splintered. Moated farms and straggling villages lay ruined, roofless, and gaping-walled—if they stood at all.

By night the winter moon looked on the twisted dead, the cornfields and roofless farms with white dispassion. Frost

48

mantled the trees and whitened the tents where No. 298 Prisoners of War Company crouched by the gaunt ruins of Bailleul, the town which was blown to atoms in twenty-four hours.

No longer was the night horizon lit by the fantastic spears and flashes of gunfire, the ghostly aurora borealis of the front line, no longer pin-pointed by star shells or shuddering with the thunder of guns.

In our tents and shacks outside the great barbed-wire cages which prisoned 450 Germans, newly-taken, we, the guards, shivered with cold. In their prison tents the Germans slept like sardines for warmth's sake. We were new to the ruins of that spectral town, we and our prisoners, who a month before had been fighting us. The Arctic cold smote English and German alike.

So when at the railhead to pick up post and rations, I heard by chance words of a great country *auberge*—an old posting inn of the eighteenth century—whose stables and ruined rooms were full of abandoned Queen stoves, that perfect little camp cooker, I determined to impound the lot.

Next day, late in the afternoon, after a morning of sudden thaw, I took Corporal Barr, that minute but unquenchable fighting man, and set off along a rutted road from Bailleul to the east. Flooded fields lay on either side. Rotted crops stained the soil. The smell of dead men, cold and oily, that smell which strikes to the pit of the stomach like the smell of a dead snake, was heavy on the air.

Ahead, in the afternoon sun, the road gleamed with sudden splashes and shields of light where water lay. Two kilometres, near enough three, and we came to the standing archway of the *auberge*. The yellow walls of what had been a fine old Flemish inn stood windowless, gazing like dead eyes over the fields of the dead. Bullets had sieved its walls. Shells had shattered the roof where rafters and roof tree stood stark as the ribs of a skeleton.

49

Under the great arch which had echoed to the clatter of coach wheels and rung with the guttural cries of Walloon and Flamande farmers, the courtyard, with its mighty midden, showed a four-square array of stables, sheds, barns, cartsheds and coach-houses. Doors sagged on broken hinges and sandbags filled empty windows.

Within were wooden bunks, the black ashes of long-cold fires, rusty dixies and mouldy webbing, mildewed bully and Maconochie tins—and Queen stoves!

We found at least a score—enough to warm our pitiful shacks and spare one or two for the prisoners. I told Corporal Barr to bring a party of prisoners next day and remove the lot.

That dour and unimpressionable little man with the square, short body, the beetling black eyebrows and steady eyes— a soldier among the best of them—said "Aye". He was being loquacious.

Then we started back. It was, maybe, four to four-thirty and far from dark. In the sunset the sky had cleared to a wide band of apple-green fading into pink. Overhead high clouds caught a sudden ethereal sheen of crimson and flamingo. The heavens were alight above the stricken earth. On our left fields lay waterlogged and gleaming—lake beyond miniature lake.

On the right a low upland swept up to a torn, fantastic wood of larch and birch. The thin trees were twisted into grotesque shapes by shell blast. It was a Hans Andersen wood of Arthur Rackham trees through whose sun-reddened trunks we could see cloud masses lit with a Cuyp-like glow.

Suddenly, as we splashed through the sunset pools of that deserted road, German cavalry swept out of the wood. Crouching low over their horses' withers, lance-tips gleaming, red pennants flying, they charged out of that spectral wood—a dozen or more German Uhlans in those queer high-topped hats which they had worn in the dead days of

The Spectral Cavalry

1914. I saw horses, men, lances, and flickering pennons clear and sharp in the level sun.

And up the slope to meet them galloped French dragoons —brass cuirasses flashing, sabres upswung, heavy horsetail plumes dancing from huge brass helmets. Fierce-moustached and red-faced, they charged with flashing sabres on heavy Flemish chargers to meet that flying posse of grey-faced men who swept down with slender lances on flying horses—the hurricane meeting the winter wind.

Then the vision passed. There was no clash of mounted men—no mêlée of shivering lance and down-smashing sabre, no sickening unhorsing of men or uprearing of chargers—only empty upland and a thin and ghostly wood, silver in the setting sun. The earth was empty. I felt suddenly cold.

I am no spiritualist, but to the truth of this vision I will swear.

I glanced at Corporal Barr. He looked white and uneasy.

"Did you see anything?" I asked.

"Aye—something mighty queer," said that non-committal little Glasgow baker. "Ssst! look! Wha's that?" he gasped. His rifle bolt clicked back, a cartridge snapped in the breech and the butt leapt to his shoulder. In a gap in the hedge on the left two baleful eyes glared at us from a dim, crouching shape. At the click of the rifle bolt it sprang to its feet—a wolf in shape and size—and loped into a sudden burst of speed.

Two rifles cracked almost as one as the grey beast splashed through the shallow floods. Bullets spurted up sudden fountains as it raced away. Not one touched it. Yet the day before I had killed a running hare with my .303 and Barr could pick a crow off a tree at a hundred yards.

The beast raced belly-low into the sunset, leaving a trail of flying water. Bullet after bullet cracked after it, missed by yards. We were both off our shooting.

No wolf was that half-starved ghoul of a beast, but one of

53

the lost, masterless Alsatian sheep-dogs of the dead farmers, pariahs of the battlefield who ravished the flesh of the staring dead.

We reached camp, shaken and oddly shy of talking too much.

Next day, at Neuve Eglise, that skeleton of a village on the spine of the Ravelsberg, I drank a glass or two of *vin rouge* at the *estaminet* of the one and only Marie, a kilometre up the road from the Armentières Road *douane*.

I asked her of the wood and the *auberge*. And Marie, forty-five and peasant-wise, said: "Ah! M'sieu, that wood is sad. It is on the frontier. A wood of dead men. In the wars of Napoleon, in the war of 1870—in this war in 1914—always the cavalry of France and Germany have met and fought by that wood. If you will go beyond the *auberge* half a kilometre only, you will find a *petite église*. There you will see the graves of the cavalry of all these wars. It is true, I tell you."

I went. In the tiny churchyard were the graves. And the headstones told the brief and bloody tales of gallant horsemen in frontier skirmishes which had played prelude to three mighty wars. And since I love a horse and revere a good rider, whether he is an Uhlan or a Gascon under Murat, a turbaned Mahratta or a red-coated foxhunter, I stood in homage for a frightened minute.

Now that is a true tale. Twenty-six years later I told it in the Second World War to a few men. A Sheffield steel man, Colonel Shepheard, listened intently. I finished on a faint note of defiance—"believe it or not".

"I do believe it," he said steadily. "I saw something of the same sort in the last war!" And he told me this astounding story in a calm, matter-of-fact voice.

During the 1914-18 War, as a staff colonel, he was travelling in a car from Hazebrouck to Wimereux. He had with him a French captain as interpreter and aide. The car passed through various villages, none of outstanding note. He took an idle interest in the flat, poplar-lined fields, the white-washed farms and grubby villages.

At Wimereux they dined and slept. And the colonel dreamed.

"I dreamed," he told me, "that I was travelling the same road again in the same car through the same villages. But with a difference. As we approached one village the car slowed down and stopped. On either side of the road were flat fields.

"Suddenly out of the earth on each side of the road rose up the hooded, cloaked figures of silent, gazing men—rank beyond rank. There were thousands of them—all cloaked and hooded like monks. They rose slowly, and every man stared fixedly at me. It was a queer, wistful, sad stare, like a dumb question or a dumb warning.

"Their cloaks were grey, almost luminous, with a fine, silvery bloom on them like moths' wings. I seemed to touch one and it came off on my fingers in a soft dust.

"I can't remember if I got out of the car or just sat and touched the man nearest me. But they stared and stared endlessly, pitifully, with a sadness which went right to my heart.

"Then, slowly, they all sank back into the ground—rank after rank of hooded men sinking into the earth, their eyes fixed on me to the last!"

He shook his shoulders with a half-shiver, half-shudder. I waited.

"Next morning at breakfast," he went on, "I told my French aide of my dream. He listened and suddenly became excited.

" 'You know the name of that village near where your car stopped?' he asked.

" 'No,' I said. 'What was it?'

" 'Crécy!' he said.

"So," said ex-staff Colonel Shepheard, "I had seen in my dream the cloaked and hooded thousands of the archers who died on Crécy field in August 1346. That," he added simply, "is why I believe your yarn."

And, to cap this tale and that of the ghostly cavalry skirmish at Bailleul, there is the tale of my friend, Major S. E. G. Ponder, the Oriental traveller and novelist, who lives at Bourne Mill, Colchester.

Major Ponder, a Regular gunner, served in the 1914-18 War in a Heavy Battery of the Royal Artillery under a Major Apultree, a red-faced, choleric officer with a sultry blue eye, a scalding flow of language and the kindest heart imaginable. He was, says Ponder, the last man on earth to see a ghost.

On a night in autumn, 1916, on the Aisne a captain whom he prefers to call "A" and a subaltern whom he calls "B" were ordered to go up the Hessian trench to the most advanced O.P. in order that Captain A should show Lieutenant B the field of fire.

"It was," said Major Ponder, "a macabre O.P. for the parapet and parados were built mainly of the bodies of dead Germans! For some reason the dead did not seem to decompose on the Somme—something in the soil. They simply looked like alabaster—very odd.

"Well, the Boche put down an extra heavy barrage that night and neither A nor B showed up. I wasn't particularly worried about them as there were several deep dug-outs they could get into.

"Next morning, about six, I was having a mug of tea in the mess—a half-buried Nissen hut—when Apultree appeared in the door. He was dead white and shaking like a leaf.

" 'Good lord, what's the matter,' I said.

" 'I've seen B,' he said queerly.

" 'He's back all right, then?' I said.

" 'No, he's dead!'

" 'What on earth do you mean,' I said.

" 'He suddenly appeared in the door of my dug-out,' said

56

Apultree, 'and I said, "Ah! so you're back to report all right!"'

" ' "No," he said, "I'm not back to report, sir, only to tell you I was killed last night." '

"And," added Ponder quietly, "he was too. Shell splinter in at the back of his ear and right through his head. Apultree had seen him all right—no doubt about that. I believe every word he said."

CHAPTER IV

"A Man I Know Told Me Of..."

THERE died on Monday, March 9th, 1936, an old friend whom I mourn. He was a man unique—the best story-teller and the best cricketer, one of the best shots, and, after Sir Adrian Carton de Wiart, the most picturesque soldier of his world and time—Lieutenant-Colonel Cyril Foley.

Poor Cyril belonged to a school now almost dead. Heir-presumptive to the Foley peerage, son of that almost too-picturesque person, the late General the Hon. Sir St. George Foley, he was not brought up to work. One was not in those days. He was a dandy and an ornament—the model of decorum, the glass of form in dress, conversation, and presence.

But although he was not taught to work, he became a very good soldier, a first-rate engineer, an unforgettable conversationalist, a cricketer who played for Eton, Cambridge, and Middlesex, an author with a humorously distinguished style and a personality whom all men loved and no woman forgot.

Now Cyril, the man who volunteered for the Jameson raid, who was Sir John Willoughby's galloper in that buccaneering foray which started the South African War—Cyril was scared out of his life by a ghost. It happened at Castle Howth, in Ireland, that ancestral seat of the Gaisford St. Lawrences which commands Howth Bay. The last, and now-dead, Lord Howth, invited him for a week-end's shooting. Castle Howth had a haunted turret wing, sheeted and shuttered. I believe they keep it shut up to this day.

No one was allowed to sleep in it. Cyril begged that he might. You had only to tell him that something could not, or should not, be done, and—provided it was fair fun—he would do it.

So they made up a bed for him in a little octagonal room, high in the turret, with barred and mullioned windows, an enormous stone fireplace, and lit only by candles in tall Queen Anne candlesticks. It was reached by a winding flight of stone steps.

The windows were shuttered and curtained. The fire of logs sputtered as gaily as a gossip writer. Not a breath of wind stirred in the room.

He started to dress for dinner. He had got as far as tying his tie in front of the dressing-table when the candles went out. He groped for matches, lit them again, and looked for the draught. There was none. The room was as empty of wind as a dictator whose bluff has been called.

Then the candles went out again.

For the second time he lit them—and saw, looking at him out of the glass, a rather pop-eyed Cyril Foley. Before he could properly appraise his own scared countenance—the candles went out again. Phhtt!

59

That was enough for Cyril. He started for the door. He could just see it in the flickering light of the wood fire.

And as he strode across the oaken-floored room in that tiny castle turret, ancient as Irish history, *something pattered behind him*!

"I opened the door, old boy," he told me afterwards, "and I walked down the stone steps—winding ones, y'know—with as good a face as I could. *But the damned thing followed me!*

"Pit-pat, pit-pat—just like that. Followed every step I took!

"There was a chap in the Skins, in the room under me, and I don't mind telling you I fairly took those last ten or a dozen steps at the gallop. And, by God, *It* ran after me!"

So now you have the lively picture of the terrified Foley, bursting into the subaltern's room beneath, in his shirt and trousers, tie under one ear, face frightened, tongue babbling out the incredible story.

" . . . And, d'y'know, the damned thing followed me step for step all the way downstairs—pit-pat—just like that. Scared the pants off me!"

"I don't wonder," remarked the subaltern dryly, looking at him. "Pity they didn't fall off. You've got your braces hanging down behind!"

The braces did not explain why the candles went out.

I remember him telling that story in my flat in Pall Mall to that fierce-moustached, bald-headed, erudite and encyclopaedic pioneer of motoring, that loquacious compendium of knowledge, Colonel Mervyn O'Gorman, the man who invented a plan—he is always inventing plans—for a vast raised road system round London which antedated the Bressey Report by eight years.

Colonel O'Gorman is a talkative and clever Irishman. As befits one who is vice-president of the Federation Aeronautique Internationale, vice-chairman of the Royal

Automobile Club, and an ornament of innumerable other learned and distinguished bodies, he is a man of meticulous observation and scientific mind, not lightly given to hasty conclusions.

This is what happened to Colonel O'Gorman. As a young man he was given to athletic pursuits coupled with an insatiable desire to explore new forms of transport—a characteristic which has lingered. So he became a bicyclist: one of the first.

One day he cycled from London to Shipton Manor, in Oxfordshire, where he was invited for the week-end. It is a long way. He arrived tired out. After dinner he retired to an early bed, so fatigued that he could barely keep his eyes open. His room was an impressive apartment, panelled and dimly lit by candles. The bed was large and low. He undressed and fell into bed. His head had barely touched the pillow before he was asleep. You will note that he was in a most unpropitious mood for ghosts.

Late in the night he awoke. His senses were suddenly alert. Something was in the room. He could hear nothing, yet that sixth sense of all Irishmen told that he was not alone in the great gloomy room. It was pitch dark. He could not see his hand in front of his face. The house was utterly still. He lay listening.

Suddenly *It* came . . . a long-drawn shuddering sigh. It ended on a sob, the sob of a tired and weary person. And the sound was within a foot of his head.

He lay like one dead, petrified with Heaven knows what apprehension. For five terror-ridden minutes he strained every nerve to catch another sound which might explain that ghastly sobbing sigh. Then, slowly, inexorably almost, *the bed moved beneath him.* Something, some grim force, was moving the very bed on which he lay. It heaved upwards . . . then subsided. And again came that ghastly shuddering sigh. Then silence.

Perhaps twenty minutes later he fell asleep. Even the

presence of that terrifying other Thing in the room was not proof against the fatigue of the day.

Hours later he woke again, every nerve tense. Something was moving in the room. Very softly *It* moved . . . a slow, sibilant, dragging sound. It was as though a tired soul was moving through eternity. And there came the thin clink of a chain. Even in death the Thing was fettered.

Then happened the most terrifying manifestation of all that nightmare night. The Thing reached the door not ten feet from O'Gorman's bed, and smote it . . . a dull heavy blow as though a pillow of feathers had been hurled against it. In the almost opaque blackness of the room he saw for one dreadful second the dim vision of a giant, formless shape reared against the door . . . a shape unlike man or beast. Then the shape disappeared. Again came that sobbing, pain-filled, terrible sigh.

Alone in that pitch-black room with the prisoned spirit, the victim of an ageless crime, he lay stone-cold with terror, not daring to stretch out a hand for match or candle. And so the dreadful night dragged on. Towards morning he fell asleep. The Thing had not made itself heard again.

He woke in a start of reawakened terror to find a footman drawing the blinds and wishing him good morning. The man turned towards the foot of the bed to take O'Gorman's clothes. Suddenly his jaw dropped. He stared at the foot of the bed with horror.

"Good Heavens, sir," he gasped, "you don't mean to say that our dog has been in here all night, sleeping under the bed. And with his chain on too! Here . . . come out of it, Bruce . . . time you were fed."

Which reminds me, for no particular reason at all, of the night when my wife and I slept in a small manor-house in Norfolk. We had stayed in that house every shooting season for many years. The month before we arrived our host's mother, a charming, elderly Scots lady who "saw things"— harmless, gentle, fairylike things, spectral rabbits and imps, ghostly birds and elves on toadstools—had died. She had reached that decorative stage of old age when she walked from room to room leaning gracefully on a thin, black, gold-topped, ebony walking-stick. Its tap-tap on the floor-boards was an everyday noise of the house.

We went to bed early. I was asleep by eleven. Somewhere about midnight two sharp taps rattled on the floor-boards of the bedroom. Two more struck the wall above my head. We both sat up, wide awake. The blows were so sharp and distinct that the echoes seemed still to ring in the room. But we heard no more.

Next morning I told my host's wife. She begged me not to say anything to her husband.

"We heard it every night for a month after she died," she explained. "But now we don't hear it at all. I expect she came to visit you because you knew her so well."

She offered to change our room for us. We refused. Since then we have stayed in the house more than once—but no more stick tappings have come in the night.

And now I will tell you of the most remarkable London ghost, the most terrifying phenomenon I have ever heard of, witnessed by two eminent and sceptical journalists—the late Ralph Blumenfeld, one of the greatest editors of this century, and Sir Max Pemberton.

It happened some years ago, when Blumenfeld was editor of a great national daily newspaper. Remarkable stories filtered into the office of a nameless Terror which haunted a set of barristers' chambers in Lincoln's Inn. The rooms had a diabolical reputation. One man had committed suicide there. Another had gone mad. Two or three had left the place, clearly scared but unwilling to risk ridicule by saying what they had seen. So the news-hawks of Fleet Street got busy.

R.D.B. arranged with the owner of the building that he and Sir Max Pemberton should have free use of the rooms for one night, that they should furnish them as they chose and print exactly what they saw.

63

So the rooms, which communicated, were stripped of furniture, carpets, and window hangings. The electric light bulbs were left naked. The windows were shuttered and closed. The communicating doors were left wide open.

And at a green baize table in the main room, the two men sat down at 11 o'clock in the evening, with a plate of sandwiches, whiskies and soda, and a pack of cards. The floor of each room was strewn thick with powdered chalk.

An hour went by. The naked electric lights lit starkly the bizarre picture of these two, seated opposite each other on spindly office chairs, the rustle of the cards the only sound in the quiet room.

Midnight came. Outside was a full moon. The trees in Lincoln's Inn stood still and brooding against the stars. White moonlight picked out roofs and chimney-pots with uncanny distinctness. The great clock of the Inn boomed the first resounding, tremulous note of midnight. Twelve times the night silence of that corner of Dickensian London throbbed to the heavy strokes of the clock.

The electric lights glared down on the two men, looking at each other with whimsical amusement. They had come prepared to take the matter in all reasonable seriousness. Midnight was the hour when things were supposed to happen. Midnight had struck. And nothing had happened.

"Well, it looks as though the visit is off," said R.D.B.

"Yes," said Max Pemberton. "Your deal." He spoke with almost comic relief.

Then *It* arrived. The outer door flew open. The two windows, bolted and shut, flew wide open. The lights went out. A strong rushing wind filled the room. Great wings beat through the rooms as though a mighty bird were passing. An overpoweringly evil presence hovered for a second.

Then the lights went on. The two men looked at each other with dead-white faces.

"Did you see anything?"

"No, but I felt it."

64

Bird Elemental

Suddenly their eyes went to the floor. There, across the white, chalk-strewn surface of each room were the enormous three-toed footprints of a gigantic bird—a bird which had taken six-foot strides. No more than that. That was all that they ever saw or felt of the Bird Elemental of Lincoln's Inn.

The building was pulled down afterwards, and no trace or sign of the Elemental which haunted the old building has been seen in the new.

This story is interesting inasmuch that it happened in London, that there were two reliable witnesses, and, above all, that the manifestation of a bird as an elemental is extremely rare.

In East Africa the natives firmly believe that Mount Elgon, in Tanganyika, is haunted by an enormous bird which flies down from the mountain top at night and carries off full-grown bucks. It may be an inherited legend from the days when that giant bird, the now extinct *Epyornis Maximus,* roamed Africa.

But that excellent and impartial authority on African natives and their customs, Mr. Blayney Percival, late Game Ranger of Tanganyika, records that he has met native after native who have sworn to the truth of the story.

To return to our London. A few years ago, in 1939, to be precise, that bland pillar of the London stage, Mr. McQueen Pope, the man who should be bound in gilt calf, printed on vellum and presented to the British Museum as an encyclo-paedia of theatrical history—this perambulating monument of stage lore, invited me to sit up in Drury Lane Theatre to watch for the ghost.

There is no doubt that they have one. Charwomen, fire-men, actors, and even members of the audience have seen it—the ghost of an eighteenth-century dandy, murdered in 1780, bricked up in a little ante-room and discovered only a few years ago when the skeleton, still clad in the shreds of a grey riding coat, was found when workmen opened up a wall.

A dagger was sticking in its ribs.

We did not see the ghost—but we did see a very peculiar bluish light which came out of the wall, flickered round the back of the upper circle, and vanished again.

The mere fact that the young man of 1780, whose ardour for one of the girls was punctured by six inches of steel, preferred not to show up, has not dimmed the belief or the enthusiasm of Mr. McQueen Pope.

"It's the most genuine ghost I know, Jimmy," he announced, with tremendous finality. "And it always appears just before a successful run. He turned up just before we began 'Glamorous Night'. Then before 'Careless Rapture'. 'Crest of the Wave' was his favourite show, for he not only appeared just before it, but several times during the run."

Could any publicity manager want a better ghost than that?

But when I talked to one cleaner in the theatre and suggested that the ghost had a good box-office sense, she looked at me witheringly and said:

"P'raps you 'aven't seen it. I 'ave! I saw 'im sitting in the upper circle one afternoon watching the stage. All empty it was too. A nice young man; slim—oh! a real good figure—and no 'at on. All in grey, just as they say.

"In fact," she wound up, "he looked so like our dear Sir George Alexander—what a 'andsome gentleman he was—that I moved up the row behind him to 'ave a peek. And then 'e vanished. What do you say about that?"

What is there to say after that?

And here let me tell of a different sort of haunting.

It happened in Essex, that county of haunted houses. There are no less than three, they say, in and about those villages called the Baddows. A year or so ago I motored through the Baddow country. I pointed to a passing glimpse of old Elizabethan gables among dark trees and said to my wife:

"That house is to let. I'll look at it on the way back."

She, a Scot from the Western Isles with the Gaelic twilight in her blood, shuddered and said:

"It's haunted. I wouldn't live in it for anything."

She had never seen that house nor knew its name, nor knew aught of it but that one fleeting glimpse at the gables through the trees.

On the way back, since I love all old houses and have no sense of decency about getting into them, I stopped and called, with my shooting partner, Sir Jocelyn Lucas. Now he is a Member of Parliament and therefore cannot tell a lie. So I call on him as my witness.

The caretaker, a cadaverous fellow with a patch over one eye, showed us into a cavernous hall, up broad, dusty stairs, to a shallow landing, whose cobwebbed windows looked on a stone-paved courtyard and, beyond it, a grass plot.

We stood on the landing for a moment and contemplated the empty stone-paved hall, the dusty corridor, the yawning doors, in the autumn gloom. It had a boding sense.

"Is this house haunted?" I asked.

"No," said the caretaker. "I ain't seen nothink. But see that bullet 'ole in the window there. . . ."

We saw. A neat, round hole, splintering outwards like a star.

"A sojer chap stood on this very landing a year or two ago an' another chap suddenly poked his rifle out o' that door over there and shot 'im dead. 'E dropped and bled where you stand, sir."

Sir Jocelyn moved hastily from a dark patch on the floor.

"That warn't the tail end of it all neither," pursued the caretaker remorselessly, mentally licking his chops. "Another sojer chap chucked 'isself off the roof and fell 'ead fust on the stone paving in the yard there. Bruk 'is blessed neck.

"An' another on 'em 'ad a word or tew with his officer on that grass patch over there, pulled a revolver out of his pocket an' shot 'is blessed self dead. Dropped right at the

69

orficer's feet. But the 'ouse ain't 'aunted. Leastways I ain't seen nothink yet."

We walked thoughtfully downstairs. In the kitchen quarters the caretaker threw open a door, pointed down dank dripping stone steps into a cavern, smelling of graveyard mould, and said ogreishly:

"Cellars. They run for ever under this 'ere old 'ouse. Ha! out under the grounds tew. Like to go down 'em? The electric light's orf but you can strike matches."

"No," we said. I beat Jocelyn to it by a split second.

"Ha! Yew oughter! There's an old room down there with a great old iron door, two or three inches thick. Bin locked for years. No one *can* open that there door. The army tried with blow lamps. No cop. *Gawd knows* what's in there. . . . Go on. Go and 'ave a look at it. It ain't 'aunted. Leastways I ain't seen nothink yet."

We went away, leaving the dark red, old house, within its high walls, shadowed by huge dripping trees, its paths overgrown, its ponds green and grey with sodden muck, its windows mute with their tale of three violent deaths, its caretaker, who lives there alone and, so far, "ain't seen nothink"—yet!

I spent a night, under the harvest moon of 1939, in Borley Rectory, which is on the Suffolk-Essex border. It is, they say, "the most haunted house in England". The late Mr. Harry Price, who was the Honorary Secretary of the Psychical Research Society, wrote a book about it under that title. They will tell you that an uneasy spirit throws things about in the Rectory. Doors open and shut. Footsteps ring where no feet walk. Bloody fingermarks appear, suddenly, on the dining-room walls, oozing blood. And there are one or two lighter sides.

Some years ago Borley Rectory was burnt out.

I went into the roofless room, taking a friend and a double-barrelled gun. We found no bloody fingerprints downstairs. We stood at the foot of the staircase and looked up it to a

landing and passage where wallpaper flickered in tattered
streamers and the moon made shifting shadows.

"Let's go upstairs," I suggested to my friend, who is young
and a soldier. He shuddered.

"Not for anything. There's Something up the top of those
stairs. It's watching us. I can feel It. I can damn nearly
see It—huge and black. Something squatting."

I raised my gun.

"Come outside," he said. "For God's sake don't shoot. I
don't like it. In any case, you'll fetch the neighbours, and
we shall get into trouble for being here."

Now there are no neighbours near to Borley Rectory, but
an old empty church and a farmhouse. But we went outside.
We stood under a tree in the bright moon and looked at the
black, staring, empty windows of the house that no one could
live in for long. And Something seemed to be watching us,
malevolently, from those eyeless windows.

Then It shot between my legs. I felt its harsh bristles, its
snaky undulating muscles. It was a black cat. It went into
the house with a bound. And it did not come out again.

Now one can put what construction one likes on that.
Harvest mice are the likeliest. But when, a year later, I met
a man whose London newspaper had sent him to spend an
inquisitive night at Borley he said:

"I wouldn't go up those stairs for a fortune in the dark.
There's Something very odd in the upper regions. I stood
outside and watched the house—and, do you know, a damn
great black cat came between my legs like a bullet and went
into the house like a shot out of a gun. It never came out
again. And when I asked at the farm they said they had no
black cats. No one round there has a black cat. But anyone
who stands in that garden at night always sees that cat go
into the house. It's a spook! That's what I think."

So do I.

Newspapermen are not usually superstitious. They believe
in beer, tobacco, and expense sheets. They are alive to

the foibles of great men, the platitudes of politicians, the inanities of film stars, the illiteracy of film directors, and the gullibility of an honest and well-meaning public. But they do not believe in ghosts.

Consider then the tale told me by Mr. J. B. Wilson, who was News Editor of the *Daily Express* for more years than men's minds may run to, and is still a puissant Elder Statesman of that great organ of light and truth. Mr. Wilson I revere. He taught me my trade. I count him as a benevolent Buddha at whose feet any man may sit with benefit and learning. It is, in his opinion, the "tallest" ghost story he has ever heard in all his long experience, but the tale, whether true or not, is fantastically horrifying, and has a close affinity with similar supernatural happenings elsewhere—particularly on the Continent. I include it, therefore, with reservations.

Now years ago, between the wars, J.B. sent a reporter—and reporters are amongst the most intelligent of men—to investigate the alleged haunting of a London house. This is what happened.

It was a brick-built, Victorian sort of house in a suburban road. It had a basement and three stories above it. It looked the sort of house in which no one ever did wrong, where the milkman was always paid punctually and where the front-room on the ground floor centred about an aspidistra. One of those bald-looking houses.

Queer things went on in the basement. Knockings and bangings. Things were thrown about. People who went down there to put the milk in a cool place, or dump a sack of potatoes, were thrust aside by an invisible Something. It had an evil and a horrible atmosphere.

So at a quarter of an hour before midnight four men sat in the cellar of this otherwise highly uninteresting house in the south of England. One was Mr. Stanley Bishop, a star Fleet Street reporter and a person not lightly given to nonsense. I have counted Mr. Bishop as a friend long enough to know that his word is truth. The other three men included a psychic investigator, a clergyman, and an independent, unbiased witness.

Before them on the floor a circle was marked out in chalk. In the middle of the circle stood a wire cage with a live mouse in it. The mouse took no notice of the four men. It was too occupied with the cheese which littered the floor of the cage. Overhead electric lights glared starkly from unshaded bulbs. Every corner of the cellar was brightly lit.

Not a word was spoken. The faces of the men betrayed their thoughts. Mr. Bishop, amused, slightly cynical, a typical hard-boiled newspaperman waiting to see what new freak life was going to spring on him. The psychic investigator, frankly interested, on the tip-toe of expectation. The parson, thoughtful, almost worried. And the fourth man in a twitter of uncertainty.

In that dead silence the faint tick of a watch sounded with deadly clearness. Then, outside, the first stroke of a clock boomed out the notes of midnight. The independent witness shivered, the parson lifted his eybrows, and the mouse ceased eating.

Had it possessed eyebrows it would have lifted them. It crouched and shuddered. Then it ran wildly round the cage, like a mad thing. A sense of terrible evil filled the room. It was cold and inhuman, that sudden sense of an overmastering, dreadful Presence.

The mouse fell, kicked convulsively once, and was dead. The chill Presence had slain the tiny thing with a thunderbolt of evil will-power.

And then, as the watchers watched, the mouse, not five seconds dead, turned to rotten, putrefying matter. Its coat shrivelled, the hairs fell out, the skin peeled off, and before the fascinated, watching eyes of four beholders the small body disintegrated into slime and stinking matter. And as this thing happened, so the Presence intensified the cold

73

atmosphere of evil. The cellar became a dreadful charnel-house of the Devil . . . then the Presence faded, the chill died away, the atmosphere became almost normal.

The next night the watchers waited once more. This time the circle was occupied by a large joint of fresh beef on a platter. It was as fresh as meat can be, fit for consumption, fit to keep for a week if necessary.

And at midnight the cellar, warmed by oil-stoves, became suddenly chill. The same sense of evil pervaded the entire room. The ghastly Presence once again dominated the four watchers. And before their eyes the joint of fresh meat turned first bluish, then grey and oozing putrefaction, and finally slopped into rotting slime. The stench was unbearable.

It was then that the parson arose, a tall, white figure of dignity.

In a voice terrible with the majesty of the Church of God he spoke the solemn words of the prayer for the exorcism of devils and all evil spirits. The splendour of two thousand years of triumphant Christianity was in that solemn prayer. By bell, book, and candle, by the Word of God and by Holy Water he commanded the evil Thing which had done this deed, to begone and cease from troubling the house wherein they sat.

Since that day the House of the Rotting Meat has had peace.

Now, to go back to the beginning, this strange affair was the climax of one of the most remarkable hauntings in the whole history of the supernatural in England. For a considerable period the house had been troubled by an evil spirit, a dominating sense of something terrible and menacing. No one would stay in it. Tenants felt that their lives were in peril. Servants refused to stay. The owner seriously contemplated pulling the house down.

As a last resort a psychic investigator was allowed to try his hand. By invoking old prayers and exorcisms he claimed finally that he had located the seat of the evil spirit in a certain cellar of the house. There the magic circle was drawn. There the mouse died. There the spirit was cast out.

The late Sir Henry Segrave once told me that the only time he was really frightened by the unknown was when he saw a piano rise in the air without visible means of support. That particular little trick happened in Hannen Swaffer's flat overlooking the Nurse Cavell statue at the junction of Chandos Street and Charing Cross Road. Hannen tells me it was nothing out of the ordinary. But then he is accustomed to such things. He is not as other men.

Poor Henry Segrave was a very dear friend and I knew his beliefs and pet aversions. He was superstitious up to a point. He believed in an after-life from which it would be possible to communicate with people still living.

When he was at Daytona Beach between the wars, waiting to make an attempt on the world's land speed record, he suddenly received a message from Swaffer in England. It was a cablegram sent through a second person, and it warned him to beware of the driving belt of his car. It would probably snap at a certain number of revolutions per minute.

Now, Hannen Swaffer knows nothing about motor-cars. Even he will admit the fact. But at a seance in his house a message came through from the late J. G. Parry-Thomas, the famous racing motorist and one of the best fellows that ever walked. Parry-Thomas was killed at Pendine Sands in Wales when the driving belt of his car snapped and beheaded him while the car was travelling at over one hundred miles an hour. I told the whole story in my *Life of Sir Malcolm Campbell*.

Parry Thomas's spirit warned the medium in Swaffer's flat that Segrave's chain would snap in the same manner and at a certain given number of revolutions. Segrave had the chain taken off and tested. It snapped at the given number of revolutions. Had he been in the car he would have been killed.

75

Two years later, on June 13th, 1931, Hannen Swaffer left the bedroom of his flat to go out for an hour or two. He and Mrs. Swaffer both noticed a copy of a daily paper lying on the bed. It was folded flat in its proper sequence of pages.

Some time later they both returned. The flat had been locked during their absence. No person had been left in it. They walked into the bedroom they had left. The newspaper was no longer there. The electric light bulb from the middle of the ceiling was in the fireplace unbroken. In the next bedroom the missing newspaper lay on the bed . . . open at the page which gave the morning's news of Sir Henry's forthcoming attempt to be made that day. They took it back to the first bedroom, folded it and placed it back on the bed. The electric light bulb was restored to its place.

Half an hour later Swaffer went into the first bedroom. The newspaper had been removed to the second bedroom and again lay open at the same page as before. The electric light bulb was again in the fireplace. Soon after the telephone bell rang. It was the *Daily Express* speaking:

"Come back to the office at once, please," said a voice, "Sir Henry Segrave has crashed and is not expected to live. . . ."

I know that story to be true in fact and detail. You may make what meaning you please of it.

CHAPTER V

Some London Hauntings

HISTORIC bricks were falling in Kensington as this book was being written. The walls that sheltered Premiers and statesmen, wits and poets, great writers and high commanders, dissolved in dust which filmed the leaves of oaks and cedars that were seedlings when London was a little city, Knightsbridge was a hamlet, and Kensington a muddy village infested by footpads. For the last remains of Holland House, the last great Elizabethan private palace within the metropolis, was being pulled down in the spring of 1954 and history was blown away on the wind.

The great rose-red mansion which was the living heart of a mighty tradition stood then, a sere skeleton of magnificence, scarred by bombs and scorched by fire. The last war dealt the death blow.

The London County Council bought, from the Earl of Ilchester, the house with its fifty-four acres of woods and meadows, terraced gardens and lovely parterres for a quarter of a million pounds, to turn it into a permanent open space.

Within the heart of this unique pleasance there will still stand the remains of the ballroom and the stately arcades of one front. Almost all the rest was razed to the ground.

Valiant efforts and eloquent pleas were made to restore and rebuild the mansion. But the cost would have been too great, the burden on the ratepayers too monumental. What London will lack in the glory of bricks and mortar it will gain in the peace of gardens and the mystery of ancient woodlands, whose story is as old as time. The ghosts and the memories remain.

Holland Park suggests an ultra-respectable labyrinth of tree-lined streets in which gentility, not yet decayed, but hovering on the brink, still maintains those Victorian standards of which South Kensington is the arch-champion.

But the Holland Park of bricks and mortar is a mere tamed and civilised slice of that true Holland Park, whose virgin acres have never known the pick or trowel of a builder since the last woad-clad Briton pitched his skin tent on that pleasant champaign which overlooked the snipe marshes of Earl's Court and the green and quaking bogs of Fulham.

Northumberland House has gone. Above its gates, fronting Trafalgar Square, there stood, in the memory of many, the great stone Percy Lyon. The house vanished on the tide of Jabez Balfour's visions and the Lyon now gazes from the roof of Syon House across the Thames to Kew Gardens.

Devonshire House fell before the march of Americanised plutocracy in architecture. What was Lansdowne House is now a warren of flats and a club. The tale of those other mansions which once made London a city of private palaces is now dead history. Alone, Holland Park, until the war, maintained the dignity of a great private house set amid oaks and cedars, green grass and terraces and the charm of birds.

There are still owls in its oaks, pigeons nesting in their branches, still hawks that hover and still a pheasant who

78

crows when the sun sets. There are even men who say they have heard the nightingale in Holland Park.

And yet, with all this unspoiled beauty, this essence of old London, not one Londoner in a thousand has seen the house or knows a tittle of its story.

Holland House was built in 1607, a few years after the first Elizabeth had gone to her grave. Sir Walter Cope, father-in-law of Henry Rich, Earl of Holland, who took his title from Holland in Lincolnshire, was its builder. He called it Cope Castle, and it stood in the fields, at the end of muddy country lanes, far from the city walls. To reach it you travelled by horse, past the hamlet of Knightsbridge, where two medieval knights once fought upon a bridge until both were slain. Then one went by way of the village of Kensington, which, until late into the time of the Georges, was a nest of robbers, a cesspool of iniquity.

The widow of Henry, Lord Holland, married Addison, sometime Secretary of State, that star of English literature, from whom Addison Road takes its name, just as Warwick Road and Warwick Gardens are named after his stepson, the Earl of Warwick.

Addison wrote some of his best work in the rooms of Holland House. Until the bomb fell, they still preserved the old green velvet-topped table, stained with his ink splashes, on which he wrote.

When Addison was dying in Holland House, he sent for his stepson, the dissolute Earl of Warwick, whose debaucheries were Oriental. As Warwick walked to the bedside, Addison raised himself painfully on his pillows, looked him straight in the eye and said, in the slow tones of one near death: "I have sent for you that you may see how a Christian can die in peace." He leaned back and two minutes later was dead.

Leigh Hunt had a charming story of Addison. He gives us a picture of him pacing the great library which ran from end to end of the house, a hundred and fifty feet in length, and there meditating those "Spectators" which made his name. At either end of the library stood a bottle of wine on small tables, and Addison "comforted his ethics by taking a glass of each as he arrived at either end of the room".

It is a nice story, but, as a later Lord Holland rightly says: "Fancy may trace the exquisite humour which enlivens his papers to the mirth inspired by wine; but there is too much sober good sense in all his lucubrations, even when he indulges more in pleasantry, to allow us to give implicit credit to a tradition invented, probably as excuse for intemperance, by such as can empty two bottles of wine, but never produce a 'Spectator' or a 'Freeholder'."

Addison's ghost is not one of those who haunt the pathetic ruins of Holland House, but if you go back to that pleasant and credulous gossip, John Aubrey, you will find this story:

"The beautiful Lady Diana Rich, as she was walking in her father's garden at Kensington, to take the fresh air before dinner, about 11 o'clock, being then very well, met with her own apparition, habit and everything, as in a looking-glass. About a month after, she died of the small-pox. And it is said that her sister, the Lady Elizabeth Thynne, saw the like of herself, before she died. This account," he adds, "I had from a person of honour."

Now this story may be true or not, but it is an odd fact that, thirty or more years ago, the Dowager Lady Ilchester told my mother that the ghost of a woman had been seen in the grounds more than once.

There is a grimmer ghost, the figure of Lord Holland, who walks on certain nights with his head beneath his arm. It is an ironic haunting, for if any man deserved to lose his head it was Lord Holland.

The Hollands were succeeded by Charles James Fox, who, when he became a peer, also took his title from the house. It is the only time that a London house has provided an hereditary title. Fox lived but little in his great house, for as all history knows, he drank, gambled, and dwelt in clubs.

Ghosts of Holland Park

His father, Henry Fox, "the elder Fox", the bitter opponent of Lord Chatham, made a mark on history which will outlast the memory of Holland House. Better than all his political achievements, I like that story of how, when he lay dangerously ill, George Selwyn, whose greatest work perhaps, to my mind, was that he helped to found White's, called on him. Now it was well known that George Selwyn always liked to be in at the death when a friend was dying or a man was to be hanged. No public execution was complete without him.

They told Lord Holland that Selwyn had called and been sent away. "Be so good," said his Lordship, "in case Mr. Selwyn calls again, to show him up without fail; for if I am alive I shall be delighted to see him, and if I am dead, I am sure he will be very pleased to see me."

It was the third Lord Holland who created for Holland House that undying tradition which has given it a permanent place in the history of English art and literature. He was one of the last great patrons of the arts. His house and his stables were open to any man with brains. What a resounding roll there is of those who made the circle which produced a mighty epoch.

Reynolds, Lord Byron, Washington Irving, Tom Moore, Sheridan, Lord Macaulay, and Talleyrand are a few to whom Holland House was a second home.

Before the war they still showed the bedroom of Charles Fox, the chamber in which Addison died, the room where Rogers, the poet, slept, and one almost adjacent where Sheridan stayed many nights, "in the next room to which", as Leigh Hunt says, "a servant was regularly in attendance all night, partly to furnish, we believe, a bottle of champagne to the thirsty orator, in case he should happen to call for one betwixt his slumbers, and partly—of which there is no doubt —to secure the bed-curtain from being set on fire by his candle".

One could tell many more stories of Holland House. There is, for example, the delicious one of Lady Caroline

Lennox, who was ordered by her parents to come down to
dinner to meet the man they had chosen for her husband.
She obeyed, against her will, and came down—with her
eyebrows shaved off!

Then there is the tale of how a Lord Holland called on
Lord Lansdowne and showed him the epitaph he had composed for his own tombstone: "Here lies Henry Vassall Fox,
Lord Holland, who was drowned while sitting in his armchair." Lord Holland died soon after, in his armchair as he
had prophesied, of water on the chest.

Then there was the affair of the eccentric Lord Camelford, who fought his fatal duel in the grounds with Mr. Best.
He insisted on fighting because he had heard that Mr. Best
was the best shot in England. Camelford missed, but Mr.
Best did not. Camelford fell, mortally wounded, and calling
Best to him, grasped his hand and gasped: "I am a dead
man! You have killed me, but I freely forgive you."

That affair was a little different in its ending to the duel
fought in the same grounds between Mr. Fox and Mr. Adam.
There had been a great hullabaloo, a few weeks before, about
the bad quality of the ammunition served out to the navy.
Fox received Adam's bullet in the chest, but it did not kill
him. "By gad, sir," exclaimed Fox, "it would have been all
over with me if we had not charged our pistols with Govern-
ment powder!"

You will observe that the history of Holland House con-
tains all the elements which make history worth reading.

CHAPTER VI

Ghosts of the West

THE west, the ancient Kingdoms of Merlin and King
Arthur, and the principalities of the chieftains of Wales,
is the immemorial home of fairies and pixies, of hauntings
and warnings, of white and gliding figures and spirit voices
in the night.

One could fill a book with the legends of Cornwall alone,
and two books with those of Wales and, for that matter, a
whole library with the fantasies and wild imaginings which
take their root, as by right, in the bogs and glens and amid
the misty hills of Ireland.

It is not my business to venture far into realms of Irish
folk-lore, for that is a territory of its own, but I cannot for-
bear to give here the diverting and highly up-to-date tales of

a latter-day familiar of the fairies, 88-year-old Mrs. Annie Mooney, of Farushklin by Glenariffe in County Antrim.

Mrs. Mooney told her story to my friend, Mr. Rushworth Fogg, a well-known Fleet Street journalist, formerly on the *Daily Mail,* and later assistant editor of Reuter features. He was the author of many of the official answers for the B.B.C. Brains Trust, and, twenty years ago, hit the headlines of the *Daily Dispatch* with his story of Gef, the Talking Mongoose of Doarlish Cashen, Isle of Man.

Mr. Rushworth Fogg, writing of Mrs. Mooney, says:

It's true they cóuld be "very vicious in their ways". So Annie's mother told her that when anybody mentioned the fairies she should "speak respectful" of them and say, "Fair may they come and fair may they go."

But that's about three-quarters of a century ago, and the neat little white-haired old lady in rimless spectacles is quite sure that the "gentle people" have abandoned North Antrim.

"I never saw a fairy," she admitted, a little regretfully, as she let me into the little cottage at Cushendall, where she lives all alone. "But I heard them, always in the night time, and I saw the light up in the hills. I would be about twelve, I should think, then. It was like violin music, more than one violin, but it was tunes I didn't know and can't remember. They did used to say that the fairies lived in the little caves among the stones that came rolling down the mountain above the farm.

"But my father wouldn't believe it. He said it was all nonsense. Men are like that!"

She shook her head over such scepticism and glanced towards her wireless set. "Wireless now, that's as wonderful as fairies. It would make you believe in fairies."

Mrs. Mooney knows a good deal about wireless. Since four years ago, when she made her first broadcast about the making of the quilt which covers her bed, she has been on the B.B.C. Northern Ireland programme a number of times, usually talking about her beloved needlework, but occasionally bringing in the fairy lore of her home district. She is probably the only old lady who has rebuffed Wilfred Pickles; she steadfastly refused to

"Have a Go" on his programme, feeling that her old friends on the Northern Ireland programme might be hurt.

"There's an old saying," she told me, "that the fairies went away the night of the Big Wind.[1] I don't know when that was, but when I was a girl, nearly everybody in Glenariffe was scared of annoying them.

"If a mother went out of the house and left a small child, she'd put tongs across the cradle to protect it from the fairies. Sometimes she would put the tongs across the doorsill. They make a Cross, and nothing evil can pass. I've often seen mothers put meal and salt on children's heads to save them from being taken."

The little people preferred taking boys to girls, so in Glenariffe in Mrs. Mooney's young days, the boys were disguised in petticoats to fool them. This custom has persisted into more recent times on the islands of the west.

What happened when the fairies "took" children? Mrs. Mooney explained: "There used to be children then called 'undergrowths'. They didn't grow any bigger, and people said they were taken by the fairies when they were young. You don't see as many 'undergrowths' since the fairies left."

Had Sir James Barrie heard of this effect of contact with the little folk when he invented Peter Pan, the Boy who Never Grew Up? Mrs. Mooney, who has read and listened-in quite a lot, was interested in this suggestion of mine and thought it quite likely, "for there were fairies in Scotland, where he came from, you know, as well as in Ireland.

"Our mothers," she went on, "told us we must never eat sloes, because they were the fruits of the fairies, and we must never eat blackberries after Michaelmas Fair, which was September 28, because after that they belonged to the fairies."

Very few people actually saw them, as they rarely came out except at night. "But I once heard an old woman saying that a wee woman came into her house and asked for a bowl of meal," recalled Mrs. Mooney. "The woman of the house said, 'I don't know you.' 'Yes,' said the wee woman, 'I live in that big *skeagh* [thornbush] below the house,' and then she realised 'twas a fairy woman.

[1] "Actually it was long before her birth—1839! She called it the Bag Wand!"—R.F.

"The old people used to leave oaten bread and new milk out for the fairies. Nobody does that now, but there are still some people that believe in them yet."

Looking for Mrs. Mooney's birthplace and the hillside where she heard the music, I asked my way of a woman leaning over a garden gate by the roadside in Glenariffe. She knew Mrs. Mooney and about her hearing the music. "My own mother heard it too," she remarked, in a matter-of-fact way.

"I don't believe in them. It's all a lot of ould nonsense," put in her husband. Men, as Mrs. Mooney remarked, are like that!

But not all of them. In Cushendun, a few miles to the north, Dan Hernon, a small, tubby, ex-ship's carpenter who now works as a handyman in his native village, told me the story of a local farmer who defied the little people and suffered for it.

"They used to live in thornbushes, what we call skeaghs," explained Dan. "Well, there was a man took a farm up above Cushendun. A fine big man he was, John MacAirt, with bushy black hair and a great moustache on him. He said there was no such things as fairies, and that he'd cut down the skeagh he had on his place. They warned him, but he took an axe and chopped it down.

"Well, the next morning when he woke up, his fine moustache had fallen off on to his pillow, and when he looked into the glass his hair was as white as snow. I'm not telling you a word of a lie, for I saw it meself."

While Dan Hernon was speaking a tall, thin man in his sixties came down the sunlit village street. "Dan McKillop," said Mr. Hernon, "and he's another ship's carpenter and the only man I know, barring a little girl that's dead now, that's ever seen a fairy. Tell the gentleman about it, Dan."

"I'd be seven or eight years old at the time," related Dan McKillop. "I was driving cows up above Glenariffe and I heard some music beyant a hedge and a ditch. I climbed over the hedge in me bare feet—we didn't go in for boots and shoes much in them days—and there was a little man, as high as your knee, playing a fiddle. He had a stovepipe hat and a collar on."

"What else?" I asked.

"Begob," declared Mr. McKillop, "I never stopped to see. I run for me life!"

And there we leave the highly diverting—and who shall disbelieve them?—tales of my friend Rushworth Fogg for a very different sort of haunting on a North Devon strand. For this I am indebted to Mr. Vernon C. Boyle, of Westward Ho, who sends several highly interesting notes concerning superstitions in North Devon, which he contributed to Volume LXXXIV of the *Journal of the Devonshire Association for the Advancement of Science, Literature and Art*. In it Mr. Boyle wrote:

> My father, Vernon Boyle, born in 1859, used to speak of a mythical character, Old White-hat, who ranged the beach along the Northside, calling for a passage to Appledore. He wore a great white hat. This was always at night. He seems to have been doomed to make ropes out of sand in amongst the Dunes. Capt. J. R. Pile, aged 61 in 1949, has the following version:
> "Jack the White-hat was about the Crow by night. He wore a white hat with a lantern lashed to it. He seemed to be looking for something. When he hailed an Appledore boat, 'Hoy!' people would never wait, but hurry away, for they believed that anyone who went ashore to White-hat would never get away alive. There is a woman in Bideford today who is the granddaughter of Jack the White-hat, and possibly she can throw light on the story."
> This legend is connected with the one about Tracey spinning ropes of sand (*see* Lady Rosaline Northcote's *Devon . . .* p. 222).
> The Crow is the south point of Braunton Burrows, between Taw and Torridge.

Mr. Vernon C. Boyle mentions another being which haunts the North Devon coast; it is a giant bogy, with which his mother (from Parracombe) used to scare the children. Mr. C. A. Shepherd, of Brixham, has also heard of it, and it seems related to the "Cankobobus" mentioned by "Q" in *Troy Town*.

Mr. Boyle goes on to give a most interesting account of what is known as the Bible and Key Divination, which I have not heard of in any other part of the country. Mr. Boyle quotes two local characters, the first Capt. J. Pile, aged 63, a fisherman, of Bideford, whom he records as saying:

I don't remember when I first heard of this but I recall that it was often brought up in parties before I was twenty. Our people had big families and the Blackmores were very fond of parties when I was a-courting one of their girls. There was no drink but it was jolly. Some cousin would say with a laugh, "Let's see if you young courting couples are going to come together" (i.e. marry).

Then a big key would be brought and all but its loop put into the Bible at the passage in Ruth i, 61. The Bible was then lashed up with twine to hold all firmly. Then my sweetheart and I had to put the tips of our forefinger under the loop and so hold the Bible suspended between us, whilst we recited the passage in unison, repeating it after the cousin. This is the passage, I know it by heart, it is what Ruth said:

"Entreat me not to leave thee, or to return from following after thee; for whither thou goest, I will go; and where thou lodgest, I will lodge: thy people shall be my people, and thy God my God: where thou diest, will I die, and there will I be buried: the Lord do so to me, and more also, if ought but death part thee and me."

Nobody was laughing while this was done; I think because the words are so beautiful and so solemn.

Whether it was nerves, or what, I don't know, but my sweetheart and I could never complete the passage before the Book seemed to slew and drop off. Yet we've been happily married forty-six years. Other people could succeed, but not we two.

Mr. Boyle's second witness is Capt. Tom Harris, aged 84, of Brixham. The captain has been a fisherman all his life, and a staunch Salvation Army man. His story relates to a time before he knew Capt. Pile. Mr. Boyle writes:

The Key was lashed into the Book at the passage in Ruth, as told by Mr. Pile, but in Capt. Tom's account it seems to have been used only to detect a suspected liar or thief, in each case a boy. The boy would be told to hold the Key himself, hanging between his two forefinger tips. In every case (three, I gathered) the boy had trembled and confessed his guilt before the passage was even begun.

There is thus no need to impute superstition to the captain. The psychological effect of reciting the solemn words were relied upon to impress the culprit strongly.

The story of the ghost of Powis Castle, the great feudal stronghold of Castell Coch, or "The Red Castle" on the borders of Shropshire and Montgomeryshire, has often been quoted, and misquoted, but a member of Lord Powis's family assures me that there is every reason to believe that it is true.

Probably the fullest and most authentic account of it was given by Mr. J. C. Davies in that extremely rare book, seldom obtainable outside libraries and private collections, *The Folklore of West and Mid Wales*. This was published in 1911 by The Welsh Gazette Office, 26 Bridge Street, Aberystwyth, who have very kindly given me permission to use these extracts. There Mr. Davies writes:

It had been for some time reported in the neighbourhood (of Powis Castle) that a poor unmarried woman, who was a member of the Methodist Society, and had become serious under their ministry, had seen and conversed with the apparition of a gentleman, who had made a strange discovery to her. Mr. Hampson (a preacher among the Methodists about the end of the eighteenth century) being desirous to ascertain if there was any truth in the story, sent for the woman, and desired her to give him an exact relation of the whole affair from her own mouth, and as near the truth as she possibly could.

She said she was a poor woman, who got her living by spinning hemp or line; that it was customary for the farmers and gentlemen of that neighbourhood to grow a little hemp or line in a corner of their fields for their own consumption, and as she was a good hand at spinning the materials, she used to go from house to house to inquire for work; that her method was, where they employed her, during her stay, to have meat, and drink, and lodging (if she had occasion to sleep with them), for her work, and what they pleased to give her besides.

Among other places, she happened to call one day at the Welsh Earl of Powis's country seat, called Redcastle, to inquire for work, as she usually had done before. The quality were at this time in London, and had left the steward and his wife, with other servants, as usual, to take care of their country residence in their absence. The steward's wife set her to work, and in the evening told her that she must stay all night with them, as they had more work for her to do the next day.

When bedtime arrived, two or three servants in company, with each a lighted candle in her hand, conducted her to her lodging. They led her to a ground room, with a boarded floor, and two sash windows. The room was grandly furnished, and had a genteel bed in one corner of it. They had made her a good fire, and had placed her a chair and a table before it, and a large lighted candle upon the table. They told her that was her bedroom, and that she might go to sleep when she pleased. They then wished her a good night and withdrew altogether, pulling the door quickly after them, so as to hasp the spring-sneck in the brass lock that was upon it.

When they were gone, she gazed awhile at the fine furniture, under no small astonishment that they should put such a poor person as her in so grand a room, and bed, with all the apparatus of fire, chair, table, and a candle. She was also surprised at the circumstance of the servants coming so many together, with each of them a candle. However, after gazing about her some little time, she sat down and took a small Welsh Bible out of her pocket, which she always carried about with her, and in which she usually read a chapter—chiefly in the New Testament—before she said her prayers and went to bed.

While she was reading she heard the door open, and turning her head, saw a gentleman enter in a gold-laced hat and waistcoat, and the rest of his dress corresponding therewith. I think she was very particular in describing the rest of his dress to Mr. Hampson, and he to me at the time, but I have now forgot the other particulars. He walked down by the sash-window to the corner of the room and then returned. When he came to the first window in his return (the bottom of which was nearly breast high, he rested his elbow on the bottom of the window and the side of his face upon the palm of the hand, and stood in that leaning posture for some time, with his side partly towards her. She looked at him earnestly to see if she knew him, but, though from her frequent intercourse with them, she had a personal knowledge of all the present family, he appeared a stranger to her. She supposed afterwards that he stood in this manner to encourage her to speak; but as she did not, after some little time he walked off, pulling the door after him as the servants had done before.

She began now to be much alarmed concluding it to be an apparition, and that they had put her there on purpose. This was really the case. The room, it seems, had been disturbed for a long time, so that nobody could sleep peacably in it, and as she passed for a very serious woman, the servants took it into their heads to put the Methodist and Spirit together, to see what they could make of it. Startled at this thought, she rose from her chair, and kneeling down by the bedside, commenced to say her prayers.

While she was praying he came in again, walked round the room, and came close behind her. She had it on her mind to speak, but when she attempted it she was so very much agitated that she could not utter a word. He walked out of the room again, pulling the door after him as before.

She begged that God would strengthen her and not suffer her to be tried beyond what she could bear. She recovered her spirits, and thought she felt more confidence and resolution, and determined if he came in again she would speak to him.

He presently came in again, walked round and came behind her as before; she turned her head and said:

"Pray, sir, who are you, and what do you want?"

He put up his finger, and said, "Take up the candle and follow me, and I will tell you."

She got up, took up the candle, and followed him out of the room. He led her through a long boarded passage till they came to the door of another room, which he opened and went in. It was a small room, or what might be called a large closet.

"As the room was small, and I believed him to be a Spirit," she said, "I stopped at the door; he turned and said, 'Walk in, I will not hurt you.' So I walked in.

"He said; 'Observe what I do.'

"I said, 'I will.'

"He stooped, and tore up one of the boards of the floor, and there appeared under it a box with an iron handle in the lid.

"He said, 'Do you see that box?'

"I said, 'Yes, I do.'

"He then stepped to one side of the room, and showed me a crevice in the wall, where he said a key was hid that would open it.

"He said, 'This box and key must be taken out, and sent to the Earl in London' (naming the Earl, and his place of residence in the city). He said, 'Will you see it done?'

"I said, 'I will do my best to get it done.'

"He said, 'Do, and I will trouble the house no more.'

"He then walked out of the room and left me. [He seems to have been a very civil Spirit, and to have been very careful to affright her as little as possible.] I stepped to the room door and set up a shout. The steward and his wife, and the other servants came to me immediately, all clung together, with a number of lights in their hands. It seems they all had been waiting to see the issue of the interview betwixt me and the apparition. They asked me what was the matter?

"I told them the foregoing circumstances, and showed them the box. The steward durst not meddle with it, but his wife had more courage, and with the help of the other servants, lugged it out, and found the key."

She said by their lifting it appeared to be pretty heavy, but that she did not see it opened, and, therefore, did not know what it contained; perhaps money, or writings of consequence to the family, or both.

They took it away with them, and she then went to bed and slept peaceably till the morning. It appeared afterwards that they sent the box to the Earl in London, with an account of the manner of its discovery and by whom.

The Earl sent down orders immediately to his steward to inform the poor woman who had been the occasion of this discovery, that if she would come and reside in his family, she should be comfortably provided for, for the remainder of her days; or, if she did not choose to reside constantly with them, if she would let them know when she wanted assistance, she should be liberally supplied, at his Lordship's expense, as long as he lived.

And Mr. Hampson said it was a known fact in the neighbour-hood that she had been so supplied from his Lordship's family from the time the affair was said to have happened, and continued to be so at the time she gave Mr. Hampson this account.

Another ghost, which one feels the Welsh may fairly claim as their own, and one equally as authentic as the Ghost of Powis Castle, is the apparition of the Ghostly Lady who was said to haunt H.M.S. *Asp*, an Admiralty survey vessel, based on Pembroke Dockyard, which did much survey work on the Welsh coast in the sixties and seventies. Old seamen in Pembroke Dock still speak of the *Asp* and its ghost with undoubted awe. The *Pembroke County Guardian*, on February 16th, 1901, in pursuit of this ghost, unearthed and republished the following letter written to the editor on March 15th, 1867, by Captain Aldridge, R.N., former Commander of the *Asp*. Captain Aldridge wrote:

March 15th, 1867.

My dear Sir,

I herewith readily comply with your request as far as I am able, respecting the unaccountable "apparition" on board my ship. Call it ghost or what you will, still I assure you that which I am going to relate is what really did take place, and much as I was, and am, a sceptic in ghost stories, I must confess myself completely at a loss to account by natural causes for that which did actually occur. Many years having elapsed since I retired from active service, I am unable to recollect all the dates with exactness, but I will give them as far as I can remember them.

In the year 1850, the *Asp* was given me by the Admiralty as a surveying vessel. On taking possession of her, the Superintendent of the Dockyard, where she lay remarked to me, "Do you know, Sir, your ship is said to be haunted, and I don't know if you will get any of the Dockyard men to work on her." I, of course, smiled, and I said, "I don't care for ghosts, and dare say I shall get her all to rights fast enough."

I engaged the shipwrights to do the necessary repairs to the

95

vessel, but before they had been working in her a week they came to me in a body and begged me to give the vessel up as she was haunted and could never bring anything but ill-luck. However, the vessel was at length repaired, and arrived in safety in the River Dee, where she was to commence her labours. After my tea in the evening, I generally sat in my cabin and either read to myself or had an officer of mine (who is now master of the *Magician*) to read aloud to me: on such occasions we used frequently to be interrupted by strange noises, often such as would be caused by a drunken man or a person staggering about, which appeared to issue from the after (or ladies') cabin.

The two cabins were only separated from each other by the companion ladder, the doors faced each other, so that from my cabin I could see into the after one. There was no communication between either of them and the other parts of the ship, excepting by the companion ladder, which no one could ascend or descend without being seen from my cabin. The evening shortly after our arrival in the Dee, the officer I mentioned was reading to me in my cabin when all at once his voice was drowned by a violent and prolonged noise in the aft cabin. Thinking it must be the steward he called out, "Don't make such a noise, steward," and the noise ceased. When he began to read again the noise also recommenced. "What are you doing, steward—making such a —— noise for?" he cried out, and taking the candle rushes into the next cabin. But he came back quicker than he went, saying there was nobody there.

He recommended reading, and once more began the mysterious noise. I felt sure there was some drunken person there whom my officer had overlooked, and accordingly rose and looked myself, and to my very disagreeable surprise found the cabin empty!

After this evening, the noises became very frequent, varying in kind and in degree. Sometimes it was as though the seats and lockers were being banged about, sometimes it sounded as though decanters and tumblers were being clashed together. During these disturbances the vessel was lying more than a mile off shore.

One evening I and the above named officer went to drink tea at a friend's house at Queen's Ferry, near Chester, the vessel at the time being lashed to the lower stage opposite Church's Quay. We returned on board together about 10 p.m. While descending the companion ladder, I distinctly heard someone rush from the after

96

cabin into the fore cabin. I stopped the officer who was behind me at the top of the ladder and whispered to him, "Stand still, I think I have caught the ghost."

I then descended into my cabin, took my sword, which always hung over my bed, and placed it drawn in his hand saying; "Now ——, allow no one to pass you; if anyone attempts to escape cut him down, I will stand the consequences."

I then returned to the cabin, struck a light and searched everywhere, but nothing could I find to account for the noises I had heard, though I declare solemnly that never did I feel more certain of anything in my life than that I should find a man there. So there was nothing to be done but to repeat for the hundredth time; "Well, it is the ghost again!"

Often when lying in my bed at night I have heard noises close to me as though my drawers were being opened and shut, the top of my washing-stand raised and banged down again, and a bed which stood on the opposite side of my cabin, pulled about; while of an evening I often heard while sitting in my cabin a noise as though a percussion cap were snapped close to my head; also very often (and I say it with godly and reverential fear) I have been sensible of the presence of something invisible about me, and could have put my hand, so to say, on it, or the spot where I felt it was; and all this occurred, strange to say, without my feeling in the least alarmed or caring about it, except so far that I could not understand or account for what I felt and heard.

One night, when the vessel was at anchor in Martyn Roads, I was awoke by the quartermaster calling me and begging me to come on deck as the look-out man had rushed to the lower deck, saying that a figure of a lady was standing on the paddle box pointing with her finger to Heaven. Feeling angry, I told him to send the look-out man on deck again and keep him there till daybreak, but in attempting to carry my orders into execution the man went into violent convulsions, and the result was I had to go myself upon deck and remain there till morning.

This apparition was often seen after this, and always as described with her finger pointing towards Heaven.

One Sunday afternoon while lying in the Haverfordwest river opposite to Lawrenny, the crew being all on shore, and I being at church, my steward (the only man on board) whilst descending the

97

companion ladder was spoken to by an unseen voice. He immediately fell down with fright, and I found his appearance so altered that I really scarcely knew him!

He begged to be allowed his discharge and to be landed as soon as possible, to which I felt obliged to consent as he could not be persuaded to remain on board for the night.

The story of the ship being haunted becoming known on shore, the clergyman of Lawrenny called on me one day and begged me to allow him to question the crew, which he accordingly did. He seemed very much impressed by what he heard; he seemed to view the matter in a serious light and said that his opinion was that "some troubled spirit must be lingering about the vessel".

During the years that I commanded the *Asp* I lost many of my men who ran away on being refused their discharge, and a great many others I felt forced to let go, so great was their fear, one and all telling me the same tale, namely that at night they saw the transparent figure of a lady pointing with her finger up to Heaven. For many years I endeavoured to ridicule the affair as I was often put to considerable inconvenience by the loss of hands, but to no purpose. I believe that when the officers went out of the vessel after dark, none of the crew would have ventured into the cabin on any account.

One night I was awoke from my sleep by a hand, to all sensations, being placed on my leg outside the bedclothes. I lay still for a moment to satisfy myself of the truth of what I felt, and then grabbed at it, but caught nothing. I rang my bell for the quartermaster to come with his lantern, but found nothing.

This occurred to me several times, but on one occasion as I lay wide awake a hand was placed on my forehead. If ever a man's hair stood on end mine did then. I sprang clean out of bed: there was not a sound. Until then I had never felt the least fear of the ghost or whatever you like to call it. In fact I had taken a kind of pleasure in listening to the various noises as I lay in bed, and sometimes when the noises were very loud I would suddenly pull my bell for the look-out man and then listen attentively if I could hear the sound of a footstep or attempt to escape, but there never was any, and I would hear the look-out man walk from his post to my cabin when I would merely ask him some questions as to the wind and weather.

At length in 1857, the vessel requiring repairs, was ordered alongside the dockyard wall at Pembroke. The first night the sentry stationed near the ship saw (as he afterwards declared) a lady mount the paddle box holding up her hand towards Heaven. She then stepped on shore and came along the path towards him when he brought his musket to the charge "who goes there?" But the figure walked through the musket, upon which he dropped it and ran for the guard-house. The next sentry saw all this take place and fired off his gun to alarm the guard. The figure then glided past a third sentry who was placed near the ruins of Pater old Church, and who watched her, or it, mount the top of a grave in the old churchyard, point with her finger to Heaven, and then stand till she vanished from his sight.

The sergeant of the guard came with rank and file to learn the tale, and the fright of the sentries all along the Dockyard wall was so great that none would remain at their post unless they were doubled, which they were, as may be seen by the "Report of guard" for that night.

Singularly enough, since that, the ghost has never been heard of again on board the *Asp,* and I never heard the noises which before had so incessantly annoyed me.

The only clue I could ever find to account for my vessel being haunted is as follows: Some years previously to my having her, the *Asp* had been engaged as a mail packet between Port Patrick and Donaghadee. After one of her trips, the passengers having all disembarked, the stewardess on going into the ladies' cabin found a beautiful girl with her throat cut lying in one of the sleeping berths quite dead! How she came by her death no one could tell and, though, of course, strict investigations were commenced, neither who she was nor where she came from or anything about her was ever discovered.

The circumstances gave rise to much talk, and the vessel was remanded by the authorities, and she was not again used until handed over to me for surveying service. Here ends my tale, which I have given in all truth. Much as I know one gets laughed at for believing in ghost stories you are welcome to make what use you please with this true account of the apparition on board the *Asp.*

Many of the Welsh ghost stories quoted by Mr. J. C. Davies and others bear, if not all the marks of authenticity, at least the honourable scars of antiquity. There is scarcely a valley or hill, a mountain pass or ancient wood clinging to its scarred hillside which has not its legend of the fairies, the Tylweth Teg, or of witches or hauntings or ghostly voices in the night.

And if you have walked alone in the mist or in the dusk of evening down a manless hillside, with the croak of ravens hollow in the gloom and passed through the glimmering aisles of an ancient wood of twisted birches and mountain ash, where long beards of silvery moss swing in the damp wind and no bird sings, you will not doubt that such places breed ghosts and visions.

Those who live in the solitudes of the mountains, whether in West Wales or Wester Ross, whether on a Hebridean Isle or amid the shining seas of many-coloured grasses which cover an Irish bog, become creatures of fantasy, the prey to imaginings born of the wild magic of the scenery about them.

We may allow all this, but now and then, particularly when the teller is a Welshman or an Irishman, the credible becomes the incredible, the possible the rankly impossible. There is always the man who will invent a ghost story simply for the importance it bestows upon him as the teller. Such a one was the vivid Celt who, telling Mr. J. C. Davies of a spirit he had encountered on horseback, launched into the following version of a story which has been told in differing forms in almost every country in the world. Said this Welsh Ananias:

I was going home one evening from my work from Ros y Wlad, and had to go through Rosmerherin. That place you know is a terrible spot for its ghosts. People say that they are seen there in broad daylight. As to myself I did not see them in the daytime, but many a time was I kept there all night by Jack-a-Lanterns.

I saw a ghost in the form of a cat there also, and when I began to strike him he disappeared in a blazing fire. But now for the gentleman. I was near the spot where I had seen the cat when I heard the sound of a horse coming after me. I jumped one side to make room for him to pass; but when he came opposite me he did not go forward a single pace faster than myself. When I went on slowly, he went slowly; when I went fast, he went fast. "Good night," said I at last, but no answer. Then I said it was a very fine night, but the gentleman on horseback did not seem to take any notice of what I said. Then thinking that he might be an Englishman (the man was speaking in Welsh), I said in English "Good night", but he took no notice of me still.

By this time I was beginning to perspire and almost ready to fall down with fright, hoping to get rid of him, as I now perceived that he was the Devil himself appearing in the form of a gentleman. I could think from the sound of the saddle and the shining stirrups that the saddle was a new one. On we went along the dark narrow lane till we came to the turnpike road, when it became a little lighter, which gave me courage to turn my eyes to see what kind of a man he was. The horse looked like a soldier's horse, a splendid one, and his feet like the feet of a calf, without any shoes under them, and the feet of the gentleman in the stirrups were also like the feet of a calf. My courage failed me to look what his head and body were like.

On we went till we came to the cross-road. I had heard many a time that a ghost leaves everybody there. Well, to the cross-road we came. But ah! I heard the sound of the ground as if it were going to rend, and the heavens going to fall upon my head; and in this sound I lost sight of him (the Spirit). How he went away I know not, nor the direction he went.

We may dismiss this amusing vapouring for what it is worth, but no one can disregard the two stories related to me in a letter by Mr. J. M. Watkins, of Great House, Llantilio Pertholey, near Abergavenny, Monmouthshire. Mr. Watkins writes:

With reference to your requests for legends in *The Western Mail*, I can give you a number; some, however, are real. The first I will relate is the one of the cobbler in the woods of Rowlestone in South Herefordshire. My father used to stay with his grandparents on a remote farm in South Herefordshire and in this particular wood, which was in a dingle, a small stream ran through the middle. At dead of night a sound exactly the same as of a cobbler tapping shoes would plainly be heard, and grown-ups as well as children were terrified to go anywhere near the place at night. Children in the area who misbehaved were often threatened that they would be taken to the cobbler if they did not mend their ways. Of recent years nothing has been heard of the phenomena.

The next story I have to relate is something that my father actually saw. He is a well-known Monmouthshire miller and still operates the old watermill known as Imley Mills. My mother, who was a devout Roman Catholic was at home this night with us when my father took a walk along the railway line to a remote spot, about a quarter of a mile away to a place often frequented by courting couples in the summer time.

It was late November at the time and a very dark night. When he came to the spot he walked up the railway embankment and looked over on to the spot and saw a most beautiful lady dressed in white. He thought at first that it was a local school teacher who often frequented the spot in summer with her boy friend. To his amazement the figure started to glide slowly away.

He climbed through the wire fence as he could see that this was out of the ordinary. The figure kept out of his reach and disappeared in the corner of the field which adjoins the millstream and no human figure could have got away in like manner. When he arrived back in the house he had no need to tell us that he had seen something not of this world. His hair stood up and he was obviously frightened, although usually a man with cast-iron nerves.

My mother kept calm throughout as she must have known that it was the sign of death which often appeared to the Vaughan family (she was of the same family as Cardinal Vaughan). About 5 weeks after this she died, a young woman of 36 years of age. About two years previously to this I remember her coming home after visiting her mother and she was weeping bitterly. I remember her telling my father that she heard a strange knock or knocking on her mother's front door, after he had enquired why she was crying. She forecast her mother's death which took place not many weeks after these strange happenings.

If you read the book on the *Life of Cardinal Vaughan,* he mentions in the opening chapters these strange happenings which

IN A NEW VILLA

many devoted members of the family have experienced. The
Vaughans are, of course, of the same family as Roger Vaughan
who saved the King's life at the battle of Agincourt.

Another correspondent, Mrs. Lilian Youngman of Rouge-
mont, Thorn Park Terrace, Mannamead, Plymouth, sends
me a story which she declares is true, and which has the
added and unusual advantage of having occurred, not in the
romantic surroundings of an ancient house, or on a lonely
hillside, but within the prosaic walls of a newly built villa, on
a new housing estate in Weston-Super-Mare. Mrs. Youngman, who assures me that these happenings took place in
1902, shortly after she was married, writes as follows:

> I was living in Weston-Super-Mare with my husband, a com-
> mercial traveller, and my baby girl who was nearly a year old. She
> was teething and very restless, so I took her into bed with me.
> Her father was away travelling. I had a nightlight on the mantel-
> piece to give a subdued light. Suddenly I saw the figure of a
> woman come through the closed door—walk the length of the
> room and disappear out of the window. The house was a new one
> built on allotment ground.
> I tried to find out if any tragedy had happened on the ground
> nearby—but it was a new road and all the people were strangers.
> I had a little legacy left me at the end of two years, and moved
> three doors farther up the road. This house I bought.
> The former house was soon let to another tenant, who, however,
> did not stay long in it. I asked her why she had removed to the
> other side of the road, a much inferior house—and she replied
> that her children were afraid to stay in the house by themselves.
> She said that in the room upstairs loud noises were heard like the
> lashing of a whip and the butt end of a child's gun was found on
> the floor, which did not belong to one of her children. So I con-
> clude that the form of a woman whom I had seen was a woman
> who had been murdered—and that her ghost haunted the scene
> of the tragedy.

Mrs. Lilian Youngman has a further remarkable story to
tell of an occurence which took place in the ladies' bathing

103

pool at Plymouth in 1883. The story, in her own words, is as follows:

One morning in November I went to bathe on The Hoe. I was accompanied by my school friend; we were both 14 years of age and good swimmers. It was a dismal morning—no breeze and the water very calm. We went down the grassy slope by the Smeaton Tower and down the steps leading to the bathing houses, of which we had a key of one house.

We met no one on the Hoe but at the bottom of the steps near the bathing houses I happened to look up and saw a woman looking over the wall—looking at the steps at the farther end of the pool.

We undressed, and ran round the edge of the pool and swam out to sea. We did not like the water that morning as it was too calm, so we soon returned to the edge of the pool. But instead of running round the pool we thought we would swim across the pool. We both went in together with a big splash, at the point where we had seen the woman gazing. On the way back I saw a hat floating. I brought it in. It was like the hat the woman wore who had been gazing into the pool. Then we dressed and went home to breakfast.

I did not go to school that morning, but my friend did, and during the morning a policeman came and took her to the mortuary. A woman's body had been found floating just at the spot where we had gone in with a splash. She could not identify the woman because she had no hat.

An inquest was held and it seemed this woman had been seen wearing some very lovely rings on her fingers—but the rings were missing when her body was found. The verdict was "found drowned". But I conclude that a man had murdered the woman for the sake of her rings and then thrown her body into the water at the point where my friend and I had gone in with a great splash, and this caused the body to rise to the surface; also that it was the ghost of this woman whom my friend and I saw looking over the wall.

Scotland is rich in legends of kelpies or water spirits which, in various forms, are said to haunt almost every

Highland river and loch, whilst Wales and Ireland have their own versions of the same sort of watery ghosts, but legends of mermaids on the British coast are extremely rare.

These sirens of the Aegean Sea can scarcely be blamed for having fought shy of the chill waters of the British seas. No one can imagine any mermaid, with the least esthetic care for her appearance, disporting herself, for example, on an Essex mud-flat, or basking on a Hebridean rock lashed by Atlantic rollers. The Irish have a crop of them, probably seals, if the truth were known.

Yet, there is one remarkable record, duly set out by Mr. Davies in his *Folk Lore of West and Mid Wales*, which is perhaps the fullest account extant of the alleged appearance of a mermaid on our coast. The surprising thing about it is that no enterprising publicity agent for the town of Aberystwyth has yet sought to revive this seductive lady not only as a holiday attraction, but as a counterblast to the Loch Ness Monster.

According to Mr. Davies:

In the month of July, 1826, a farmer from the parish of Llanuwchaiarn, about three miles from Aberystwyth, whose house is within 300 feet of the seashore, descended the rock, when the sun was shining beautifully upon the sea, and he saw a woman (as he thought) washing herself in the sea within a stone's throw of him. At first, he modestly turned back; but after a moment's reflection thought that a woman would not go so far out into the sea, as it was flooded at the time, and he was certain that the water was six feet deep in the spot where he saw her standing.

After considering the matter, he threw himself down on his face and crept on to the edge of the precipice from which place he had a good view of her for more than half an hour. After scrutinising her himself, he crept back to call his family to see this wonderful sight.

After telling them what he had seen, he directed them from the door where to go and to creep near the rock as he had done. Some of them went when they were only half dressed, for it was early in the morning, and they had only just got up from bed. Arriving at the spot, they looked at her for about ten minutes, as the farmer was calling his wife and the younger child.

When the wife came on, she did not throw herself down as the others had done, but walked on within sight of the creature; but as soon as the mermaid saw her, she dived into the water, and swam away till she was about the same distance from them as she was when she was first seen. The whole family, husband, wife, children, menservants and maidservants, altogether twelve in number, ran along the shore for more than half a mile, and during most of that time, they saw her in the sea, and sometimes her head and shoulders were upwards out of the water.

There was a large stone, more than a yard in height, in the sea, on which she stood when she was first seen. She was standing out of the water from her waist up, and the whole family declared that she was exactly the same as a young woman of about 18 years of age, both in shape and stature. Her hair was short, and of a dark colour; her face rather handsome, her neck and arms were like those of any ordinary woman, her breast blameless and her skin whiter than that of any person they had seen before.

Her face was towards the shore. She bent herself down frequently, as if taking up water, and then holding her hand before her face for about half a minute. When she was thus bending herself, there was to be seen some black thing as if there was a tail turning up behind her. She often made some noise like sneezing, which caused the rock to echo.

The farmer who had first seen her, and had the opportunity of looking at her for some time, said that he had never seen but very few women so handsome in appearance as this mermaid.

A gentleman of West Wales, a native of Cardigan who has written extensively on the legends and country customs of that remote and charming countryside, sends me, in a long and discursive letter, a number of notes and records which give such an everyday picture of the survival of legend and belief that I think his letter worth giving almost in full. He begins by saying that:

The Will-o'-the-Wisp or Jack-o'-Lantern is very common around here. I have seen it on hot summer nights at Cenarth, near Newcastle Enlyn; on the Cardigan Marshes (a mile outside this town), and down at Nevern, near Newport, Pembs.

North Pembrokeshire and South Cardiganshire were, prior to the first war (1914), rather given to certain superstitious beliefs. On the night of the new moon, many old people would not go out of doors (I was told). Friday the 13th—was always a "scare" day; no white flowers (especially snowdrops) allowed in the house; bad luck indeed if you saw a white horse without a rider; and of course many old mansions were credited with a ghost or two.

To hear seagulls at night, or an owl in the middle of summer, or see fewer than three black lambs in springtime, not to mention one crow or magpie, was counted really bad luck. There is still in some parts of South Wales a rhyme that goes, "One for sorrow, two for joy, three meet a girl and four meet a boy" (referring to birds when seen through a window or when out for a stroll).

The Candle Corpse (in Welsh; Canwyll Corph) has often been "seen" floating down the river, and the "Hounds of Death" (Cwn Marwolaeth or Cwn Angladd), "have been seen and heard" tearing up the street or lonely country road when someone lay very ill. And if six jackdaws or other "black birds" are seen flying around or near a house, then Death is near someone in the family.

But for the past thirty years or so, these old superstitions have "died out", the modern scientific age having disproved and dispelled so much that our grandparents regarded as "'gospel".

But one strange belief among the adult countryfolk seems to remain; if a robin or any other SMALL bird flies into a room, look out for bad news.

Silver coins are still "turned over" at sight of a new moon; parsley plants are not transplanted, a certain "tempting of Providence" if this is done, and indeed there are cases of young people having been taken ill and died, and it transpired that someone had removed parsley plants just previously.

Walking under a ladder and asking for No. 13 in a raffle, is quite common today hereabouts, and everyone reads Sunday papers; (35 years ago this brought ill luck!). Strangely enough, although Cardigan Castle goes back to pre-Norman times (under Prince Cadwgan ab Bleddyn and Prince Rhys ap Gruffydd, who tried and succeeded later to stem the Norman invasion), I am not aware of any ghost stories, though there are tales told of its "awful dungeons". William II and Edward I stayed there, and what stories are told about the old place, are surely historical.

There are, however, three places near here, which in my young days were believed to be haunted. (Today, the young folk sneer at such talk!)

These places are: David's Pool (Pwll Dafydd), on the Cardigan-Llangoedmor road; Feidir Llanduduch, on the St. Dogmells-Cardigan road; and Pentood Isaf-Troedyrhiw road, just outside Cardigan Town.

At certain spots on the above three roads, the ghost of a highwayman on a white horse has "appeared"—but strange to relate, since the end of World War I, these hauntings seem to have vanished; I recollect hearing that every New Year's Eve on the Llantrisant Town-Beddau road (between Llantrisant and Pontypridd, in East Glamorgan), the ghost of a "Dashing Cavalier" on horseback—all in white—with flashing sword and fiery eyes appeared, and it is said many old folks would NOT walk that road at night in olden days. The tale has come down from Civil War days, but the youngsters of today laugh at all these quaint yarns.

I heard my mother once or twice relate the story of a North Pembroke Squire in the early 1800's, who had hypnotic or mesmeric powers, and who, finding some poor country folk stealing potatoes from his fields, "put the 'fluence on them" and kept them digging away for a week without pause or rest, the Squire supplying the potato sacks. Many old folk, now dead, told me this story was perfectly true. Another story was about the School of Black Magic in Haverfordwest, Pembroke. (I was once informed that there were six of these Schools in S. Wales and several in Lincolnshire and the East Coast, in the late 1700's and early 1800's.)

Now, I believe the well-educated people who went periodically to "study magic" at these schools, could perform wonderful things. Here is another story:

My mother and grandmother were walking along the lonely Newport-Cardigan road one autumn evening, when "from nowhere" a well-known lady appeared and walked with them into town. This old lady had been away at the Haverfordwest School

The White Cavalier

for some weeks and yet she was able to tell my grandmother that she had lost a prayer book and that she would "put a spell" on the person who had "taken it from her pew". My grandmother begged the old lady to do nothing of the kind, and wondered how she knew, as she had told nobody outside her own family about the book. The old lady, however, said she would "compel" the thief to return the book and that on their return to town, my granny and mother would find her waiting at their door with it. And when they reached home in the dawn, the woman who had taken the prayer book was indeed there waiting to hand it back, and sobbing her heart away with remorse.

My own *personal* experience is this: I was having music lessons with a lady in Cardigan whose husband, a cripple, was reputed to have the magical sense of "location", i.e. he could tell where to find anything of value which had been lost. My mother lost a silver-back clothes-brush and that was in the winter of 1910.

I casually mentioned this to the old gentleman when, in the following summer, I had gone in to have a chat with him in his garden. At first he simply told me to have another search, but a week later, after a solemn promise to tell nobody but my mother, at least during his lifetime, he told me to put my hand in a gap in our garden hedge. I rushed home, a mile or so from his house, and pushing away the moss and weeds, I located the brush, all damp and mildewed. My mother was amazed when I told her. I kept my promise, but strangely enough, after the old chap's death ten years later, it was said that a heap of ashes was found on the floor of a small room adjoining his bedroom, and it is presumed to this day that he had burned some old books and papers on magic.

Others remember his strange "faculty" for locating lost property. I sent a detailed account of this weird experience to the National Library some years ago.

We may end these ghosts of the West with the charming story told me by Mrs. A. L. Pittaway of Forge Row, Abertillery, Monmouthshire, concerning the ghost of an amiable old gentleman who for many years haunted a cottage in Hough Wood, Herefordshire, in which Mrs. Pittaway spent many years of the earlier part of her life. The cottage lay at the side of the wood and the garden adjoined the wood. In a letter to me Mrs. Pittaway says:

> We did not mind carrying water a meadow and a half away for drinking and going a mile for oil for the lamps, but we had not been there long before we heard tapping on the window and door. Footsteps from the gate passed the window and door, then went on to a shed, and after a while the footsteps came back. They stopped at the door, and the latch was lifted.
>
> We expected someone to walk in, but the door did not open. I went to the door, there was no one there.
>
> Honeysuckle was growing by the door, and Mother said that the wind made it knock the windows and door. So she cut back the branches by the windows and door, and said, "It will be all right now."
>
> But that night, sitting around the fire, we children reading and mother sewing, we again heard the footsteps come from the gate to the window, the same taps on the window, and then the footsteps passed to the shed.
>
> Mother looked at me. We both got up and waited. The footsteps returned, and as the latch was lifted, Mother threw open the door. No one was there.
>
> It was a lovely night with the stars shining, and had anyone been there, they would have been seen. The gate was locked.
>
> A couple of evenings later when I was fetching water through the meadow, I noticed an old gentleman neatly dressed just in front of me. I thought that Mr. and Mrs. M., our neighbours, had probably got a visitor. I could see that the old gentleman was making for the other meadow where the well was situated, but instead of making for the stile, he cut across the corner of the wood, and when I got over the stile into the meadow, there he was about ten yards in front of it.
>
> I got my buckets of water, and coming back, he was again in front of me. He went through the corner of the wood again and back into the other meadow, not crossing the stile. I could not understand this at all, as the hedge by the wood was so thick that a dog could not have got through it.
>
> I told Mr. M. that I had seen his visitor, but he said that he had no visitor.

After this my mother and I often saw the old gentleman, sometimes sitting on the stile, sometimes in the meadow or the garden. We got so used to seeing him that he became part of the place. Later my uncle came to live with us and he also saw him.

We spoke about the old gentleman to the people in the village, and they at once said that he had been living in the cottage that we were in and had died there. Years before there had been a path down to the well, through the corner of the wood. That was the path he used. It was a happy little cottage, and we were very happy there with the old gentleman who could not leave the place.

That, I think, is the most charming of ghost stories, not least since it bears the unmistakable stamp of truth.

CHAPTER VII

Ghosts of the South Country

OF all the ghosts, gentle and ungentle, which walk the thyme-scented downs or cry by night for their lost souls in the darkling oakwoods, or stalk in grisly solemnity the passages and stairways of ancient mansions in the south country, there is none, to my mind, to equal the haunting of Brede Place.

Brede is one of the older, smaller, and perfect ancient manor-houses of England. A house blent of all time and all history, its stones and roofs coloured by uncounted summer suns, its timbers bleached by winters that span four centuries or more of English history.

Brede has for long been the home of the Frewen family, and I cannot do better than give the story of its haunting in the words written to me by its former owner, that great gardener and man of elegant letters, Captain Oswald Frewen, who recently sold the property to his nephew. Captain Frewen writes on March 28th, 1953:

Brede Place was inhabited by Sir Goddard Oxenbridge, "the Giant" (his effigy lies on his tomb in the Oxenbridge chancel of Brede Church, about six feet four inches tall). He ate babies, so that, as he was invulnerable to steel, the children of East Sussex and the children of West Sussex made him drunk, took him down to Groaning Bridge in Stubb Lane, and there sawed him in two with a wooden saw. To many, Brede Place is known as "The Giant's House".

It is obvious that certain Intelligent Ones, running the Free Trade racket in the 18th century, and knowing that the Moral is to the material as three to one, decided that the best defence and protection for their employees against the Preventive Men was to people Brede Place with Ghosts rather than arm their fellows with horse pistols, and readiest to hand came the legends of Gilles de Retz. (I have been told, but you know friend Gilles better than I.)

On the other hand there is a presumption that there was a holy shrine at Brede Place site of old. It is just above the old highway from Rye to Lewes, just above a little stream which hereabouts ceases to be tidal and so becomes fordable at all times, and Sir Thomas "atte Ford" inherited it. He decided to build a nice Hall-type mansion, a little before 1350 (Edward III lunched here with his Queen before embarking at Winchelsea to win the battle of l'Espagnols sur Mer). It was the usual type of Hall house, on the plan of a chamber for scullions, a hall open up to the roof, with a bonfire on the floor in the centre, and adjoining that the seigneur's apartments.

But where Brede Place differs from others (which do frequently incorporate or attach a little chapel) is that at the south end, Sir Thomas built a chapel one quarter longer than the house is broad, with a priest's apartment beyond it, completely segregated from the house, seigneurs, scullions, and all.

Now my suggestion is that Sir Thomas built thus religiously on an already holy site, and installed a holy priest for his chapel and relics. He died and his daughter Joan carried the estate by inheritance to the Oxenbridges, who remained, grands seigneurs, in ownership for some 225 years, during which time one of them built a south aisle on to Brede Church, as the "Oxenbridge Chantrey", where, as I said above, Sir Goddard and another Oxenbridge lie buried.

My point in all this archaeology and history, is to establish the "super" sanctity of Brede Place Chapel with its resident priest. Now one of the later Oxenbridges, the Elizabethan, decided to modernise his old-fashioned house in accordance with the spirit of the age, and accordingly floored over the great hall (thereby ruining it and nearly wrecking the entire building) and having done so, desired the modern (Elizabethan) type grand staircase to reach the upper floors. His best, or worst guess, was to take the eastern third of the chapel and instal it there, thus giving access to the upper priest's room, hitherto reached by a ladder in a square cell-like excrescence, as well as to the rest of the house and in particular to his grand bedroom.

So that he evicted the priest and secularised the Holier end of the chapel, and built his staircase over the shrine of the relics. The (presumably last and evicted) priest clearly damned him by bell, book, and candle, and I think has remained "earth bound" ever since, breathing hatred on any who tread those unholy stairs between 10 p.m. and dawn. He is so much more powerful than one man, that very few people will pass up or down the stairs between these times, but he is not powerful enough to impose himself on two. I have never seen or heard him, nor known anyone who has, but his *Presence* is the strongest thing I have ever felt.

In a "Dell" or "Ghyll" in the top of the hill behind the house, stood, in 1910, at its head, a very old wreck of an ash, its remaining trunk some seven or eight feet high and hollow for some seven or eight feet of diameter, out of nine or ten. To clear the site for rhododendrons or azaleas, I personally got rid of it by burning all my brushwood clearances in it for a fortnight or so on end, but the whole dell, and particularly that end of it, were so "fey" that I couldn't work in the place after *sunset*. Years later I found it so inconvenient to have to cease work at sunset and not at dark, that I took advice, was told the Presences were non-human—Elementals—and that if I told them to go away in a commanding voice, they would go.

This I tried and fearfully one evening, strode through the dell, and rather to my surprise, survived! Next morning, the acid test, I strode through again, not so fearfully. I felt Presences, but only waist high.

The third night, I felt nothing, and ever after could work till dark prevented my doing so, although at the very head of the dell, by the site of the old ash, I was never completely comfortable, or rather, I was sometimes *un*comfortable.

Going back to the house it suddenly occurred to me that I seemed to be one of those privileged beings who can lay ghosts and, successful in the garden, I would lay also the gentleman on the stairs.

I waited till 10 p.m. (it is always 11 p.m. during Summer Fool Time) felt his entry into the drawing-room, arose, went to the foot of the stairs, and using precisely the same procedure, advanced resolutely up the first tread, confident in myself and told him to "pass on, pass on, I can't help you".

I felt much Power before me, advanced less resolutely up the second tread, faltered in my "mantram"—turned and *ran*. He remained.

Years later I sold to my sister, and she has described in her book, *My Crowded Sanctuary,* all sorts of communications, all of which (unlike mine) could be the result of honest, unrealised self-deception, with the one exception of a young lady who came to her, called herself "Martha", cried, I seem to remember, because she had been so wicked as to steal in the house, so that the seigneur "hanged her on that big ash at the head of the 'Ghyll' above the house".

I don't think my sister knew of the existence of the great hollow trunk which I had burned away. She says she allowed Martha to depart altogether, and in peace. I do think she must have eased her conscience, but there are still times when I do feel her about in that neighbourhood, and so do others.

My sister made friends with "Father John" but not to the extent of getting him to verify my theory, or supply details. We always regarded the Stairs Presence as that of the last priest, and auto-suggestion can terribly easily enter into the story of "Father John" as such, but the Presence *is* still there, and I think, malevolent to all except my late mother, who would go up in the old paraffin lamp and candle days, at 3 a.m., after falling asleep over her book in the drawing-room, and when asked, "but what about the ghost?" would just say, "Oh! I don't mind them, they are all *friendly* to me."

She never denied them, and she had rescued the old house from dereliction and treated the remains of the chapel with reverence.

Captain Frewen concludes this highly interesting account, which he modestly describes as "so tardy and truncated a yarn" with the words, "My nephew has bought Brede Place, but seems to have seen or felt no ghosts to date, but he and his bride live principally in the north (unhaunted) part."

Not so far from Brede Place as the witch flies is the great forest of St. Leonards, which still covers much of Sussex in the neighbourhood of Horsham, and was for centuries the great haunt of smugglers. And wherever you find smugglers, you find ghosts and hauntings, for nothing suited the purpose of the free traders better than an apparition which kept people indoors at night. The late Miss Dorothea Hurst, in her *History of Horsham,* the second edition of which was published in 1889, says of the St. Leonards smugglers that:

Mr. Aldridge, of New Lodge (now called St. Leonards), great-grandfather of the present owner, well remembered that when he was a boy it was no uncommon occurrence for thirty or forty fully-armed men to ride up the avenue to the house, and that supper used to be spread for them in the servants' hall as a sort of blackmail which the inhabitants of lonely, unprotected houses were obliged to pay on these occasions. It was the custom of these smugglers also to take the horses from the stables, use them, groom them and put them back, and so pass on from station to station up the country towards London by unfrequented roads. It is not to be wondered at that a country so wild and lawless, should abound in legends and traditionary tales of a superstitious character.

One of these legends concerns the remarkable avenue of firs in the forest called "Mike Mills' Race". The fir trees

The Dragon of St. Leonards Forest

were of immense size, but the greater part of them were blown down many years ago, but the site of the avenue, originally a mile and a quarter long, and containing 15,000 well-grown trees, is still pointed out.

According to the legend, Mike Mills was a noted smuggler, who had defied the Devil on many occasions. Old Nick more than once tried to catch him on his midnight journeys through the forest with strings of ponies laden with tubs of brandy and bales of silk. But Mike was too smart for him.

Finally, one moonlit night, the Devil, lying in wait at the end of the avenue, surprised Mike with a band of smugglers. He immediately challenged him and summoned Mike to yield, declaring that he had sold himself body and soul.

Mike, nothing daunted, set down his tubs, looked the Devil up and down with easy insolence, and noting the old gentleman's age and nobbly knees, immediately challenged him to a race down the avenue.

"If you can catch me, Nick, before I get to the end of the avenue, you shall have me at once; if not, you shall have nothing more to do with me." "Agreed," says Nick. And, says the local legend: Away ran Mike, away ran Nick. Nick being of too hot a temperament, was soon knocked up, and Mike won the race by a quarter of a mile; from which circumstance the place was named and Mike Mills rendered immortal.

A far more potent legend, however, is that of the Dragon of St. Leonards. This is set out in an ancient document printed in 1614 in the following words:

The Legend of the Dragon of St. Leonards Forest.—
True and Wonderful.

A discourse relating a strange and Monstrous Serpent or Dragon, lately discovered and yet living to the great annoyance and divers slaughters both of men and cattle in Sussex, two miles

from Horsham, in a wood called St. Leonards Forest, and thirty miles from London this present month of August, 1614.
Printed at London by John Trundle, 1614.

To the Reader,
   The just rewarde of him that is accustomed to lie, is not to be believed when he speaketh the truth; so just an occasion may sometimes bee imposed upon the pamphleting; and therefore if we receive the same rewarde we cannot much belame our accusers—which often fals out either by our forward credulity to but seeming true reports, or by false copies transcribed from other languages which (though we beget not) we foster, and our shame is little the less. But passing by what's past, let not our present truth blush for any falsehood's sake. The countrie is near us, Sussex; the time present, August; the subject a serpent, strange yet now a neighbour to us; and it were more than imprudent to forge a lie, so near home that every man might turn on our throats, believe it, or reade it not, or reade it (doubting) for I believe, ere thou hast read this little all, thou will not doubt of one, but believe there are many serpents in England.

Farewell.

by A.R.

he that would send better news if he had it.

   In Sussex there is a pretty market towne called Horsam, near which is a forrest called St. Leonards Forrest, and there in a vast and unfrequented place, heathie, vaultie, full of unwholsome shades and overgrown hollowes where this serpent is thought to be bred, certaine and too true is it that there it yet lives, within 3 or 4 miles compass are its usual haunts, oftentimes at a place called Fay-gate, and it hath been seene within half a mile of Horsam, a wonder no doubt, most terrible and noisome to the inhabitants thereabouts.
   There is always in his tracke or path left a glutinous and slimie matter (as by a small similitude we may perceive in a snaile), which is very corrupt and offensive to the scent, insomuch that they perceive the air to be putrified with all which must needs be very dangerous; for though the corruption of it cannot strike the

outward parts of a man, unless heated into the blood, yet by receiving it into any of our breathing organs (the nose or mouth) it is by authoritie of all authors, writing in that kinde, mortall and deadlie; as one thus saith: "Nosia Serpentane est admits sanguine Pestis" (Lucan).

The Serpent or Dragon, as some call it, is reputed to be nine feete or rather more in length, and shaped almost in the form of the axle-tree of a cart, a quantitie of thickness in the middest, and somewhat smaller at both ends. The former part which he shoots forth as a necke is supposed to be about an ell long, with a white ring as it were of scales about it. The scales along his backe seeme to be blackish and so much as is discovered under his bellie, appeareth to be red; for I speak of no nearer description than a reasonable ocular distance; for coming too neare it, hath already been too dearlie pay'd for, as you shall heare hereafter.

It is likewise discovered to have large feete, but the eye may be there deceived, for some suppose that serpents have no feete but glide along upon certain ribbes and scales, which both defend them, from the upper part of the throat, unto the lower part of their bellie, and also cause them to move much the faster, for so this doth and rids away, as we call it, as fast as a man can run. He is of countenance very proud, and at the sight or heareing of man or cattell, will raise his necke upright, and seem to listen and loke about with great arrogance. There are likewise on either side of him discovered two great bunches, so big as a large foote ball, and as some think, will growe into wings, but God I hope will so defend the poor people of the neighbourhood, that he shall be destroyed before he growe so fledge. He will cast venome about 4 roddes from him, so by woefull experience it was proved on the bodies of a man and woman coming that way, who afterwards were found dead, being poysoned and very much swelled, but not preyed upon; likewise a man going to chase it and as he imagined to destroy it with great mastiff dogs were both killed and he himself glad to return with haste to preserve his own life. Yet this is to be noted that the dogs were not preyed upon, but slaine and left whole—for his food is thought to be for the most part in a conie warren which he most frequents, and it is found to be much scanted and impaired in the increase it had wont to afford. These persons whose names are heare under-printed have seen this serpent, besides divers others, as the carrier of Horsam, who lieth at the White Horse in Southwark, and who can certifie the truth of all that hath herein been related.

John Steele,
Christopher Holder,
and a widow woman dwelling at Fay-Gate.

A charming crop of Sussex witches and wizards comes to me from Mr. H. A. Lee, of Bronfay, Beacon Road, Seaford, Sussex, who writes:

My father and mother often told me these tales. They were believers in witches and wizards.

My father said he worked on a farm at Clymping, Sussex. He said the farmer was a very stern mistrustful man, so he used to get on the top of a hayrick, and spy on his workmen most days. One day he was spotted by the men. Amongst them was a wizard, so he said to his mates: "I will soon cure him of this."

He bewitched this farmer, so that he could not get down from the rick. He kept him there a couple of days and then released the spell. When he came down the wizard said to him: "Perhaps you won't want to spy on us again." And he never did.

On another occasion my father said he was with another man when they had a loaded waggon drawn by a team of horses. All of a sudden the waggon stopped. The horses pulled and pulled, but the waggon would not pull. The man used his long whip, slashing at the horses. In so doing, his whip slashed the wheel, and the waggon moved easily enough, for, from this wheel ran a hare. Where it ran was a long mark of blood. This was a witch who had turned herself into a hare and bewitched the waggon wheel so that it would not move.

On another occasion my father told me of a postman who at certain times used to meet a ghost on a dark road. He was very frightened until one day someone told him that when he met the ghost he was to say to it: "Spirit, spirit, why troublest thou me." He did this the next time, and the ghost answered him, and told him to do something about a certain grave, and then his spirit could rest. The postman did this, and the ghost was never seen again.

For several years, my mother, when I was a schoolboy, was ill every Christmas, and sometimes at death's door. As I got older these illnesses ceased, and my mother said to me that she knew my grandmother (my father's mother) was a witch, and it was she who made my mother ill every Christmas, because she had never agreed to my mother marrying my father. It was strange that the illnesses ceased as soon as my grandmother died.

My father was in Australia before he got married, and my mother always said that his mother was able to say just what her boy would do even though he was so far away, and my mother said it was true. When my grandmother died, the pillow flew from under her head right across the room as soon as the breath left her body.

CHAPTER VIII

Some East Anglian Hauntings

EAST ANGLIA, my native land of fens and the high brecks, of old manorial farms and shimmering coastal mud-flats has a sturdy population of robust ghosts. They range from Anne Boleyn, sitting headless in her coach drawn by a team of headless horses which careers madly under the moon over twenty, or it may be forty, county bridges in a night, to Black Shuck, the ghastly Hell-hound who pads the Norfolk cliff-top path and haunts the coastal road from Peldon to Tolleshunt D'Arcy on the flat seaward fringe of Essex.

Essex is full of witches and wizards. Within the memory

of living men almost every marsh village on the coast and every hamlet in the ancient country of the Roothings had its witch or "wise man". Perhaps the most famous of all Essex wizards was Cunning Murell who dwelt within the shadow of the ruins of Hadleigh Castle, where the Thames meets the marshes and the flat half-land of sea and land glimmers under the moon. There is a book about him.

Now I could fill a book, twice the length of this one, with tales of ghosts and hauntings, of horrid laughter in the night, and of footsteps that tread menacingly in half the parishes between Thames and Wash, but let me start with the ghost of Springfield Place.

Springfield is near Chelmsford. It gave its name to Springfield, Massachusetts, and the Springfield rifle. The Place was till recently the home of the Ridleys, Essex brewers. Mr. Thomas B. Ridley, of Orchard Place, Polegate, Sussex, a member of the family, has urged me to tell the story. So here it is in the unimpeachable words of that excellent county newspaper, the *Essex Weekly News* with, to follow, a long confirmatory letter from Miss Petre, of Ingatestone, a member of the family of Lord Petre of Ingatestone Hall.

The *Essex Weekly News* says, in its issue of January 1946:

A story was going the rounds yesterday that the ghost of Springfield Place had reappeared.

Springfield Place, a centuries-old house, standing close to the east end of the Parish Church, is the property of the Ridley family, but has been requisitioned by the Ministry of Supply as a hostel for girls employed by the Hoffman Manufacturing Co. Most of the girls are from Southern Ireland.

Recently, so the story goes, two of the girls sleeping on the top floor, suddenly awoke in fright. They complained that something uncanny had touched their faces. There were also reports of other strange happenings, such as of things falling.

Inquiries brought to light the fact that in years gone by, Springfield Place had the reputation of being haunted by the figure of a man, and as the ghost of those days was said to wander in that part of the house from which the latest disturbances were supposed to have occurred, that section of the building has been put under lock and key.

That is the story. So far as can be ascertained, no one has actually seen the ghost, though members of the Ridley family were told, as children, that the place was supposed to have one.

If there is a ghost, he has been very quiet since the key was turned upon him. The girls no longer worry, but sleep in peace.

In a later issue, the *Essex Weekly News* printed the following letter:

Sir,—I was very interested to read in your issue, of the ghost in Springfield Place.

In 1864 my grandparents, the Hon. Henry W. Petre and his wife, Eleanor, went to live at Springfield Place, which they occupied for 21 years. During this period the ghost was actually seen on one occasion. I cannot do better than quote from a book written by their eldest daughter, Mrs. Philip Wellesley-Colley (formerly Lucy Petre), in which she says:

"The old house is called 'Springfield Lawn', and this on account of the big expanse of mossy lawn in front of the house. There is a magnificent old oak staircase with carved banisters which is quite a feature in the interior of the house; under this there is a spacious cupboard having a secret underground little chamber, which may have been a priest's hiding-hole. The large bedroom called the Blue Room, or Ghost Room, about which there seemed a deep mystery, is panelled in oak and painted light blue. High up on one of the walls there are hinges of cupboards, which always had a mysterious significance for us, but they were never opened in our time. There were some other uncanny things in this old house, such as trap doors, dark passages and bricked-up windows.

"In August (1868) grandmother Walmesley died such a saintly death at Ramsgate. Mother was away a long time nursing her; she had a baby Nellie (afterwards Lady Young), who was very ill, with her, so had a double anxiety. Nell was still ill and feverish with her teeth. One night she was more restless than usual, and Mother took her into the Blue Room to prevent her from disturbing Father.

"Baby Nell at length was made quite content with some hard rusks to gnaw to help her teeth to come through, and then Mother began to doze; but a chuckle from the child aroused her; baby was calling out, 'Funny man, funny man!' Instantly Mother looked up to see what was the matter and beheld a hideous little man standing with folded arms and his back to the fire. A momentary act of terror made Mother cover her head with the bed-clothes; then in the next instant she sprang out of bed, but the elf had vanished. Baby kept up her 'funny man' and seemed much amused.

"Mother searched every cupboard and cranny, but no trace could she find of the dwarf; she did not like to go and wake Father, so she said a prayer and got back quietly into bed and soon fell fast asleep.

"The next morning we had a full account of the whole affair and were not in the least surprised, as it had happened in the Blue Room, the haunt of ghosts. We pestered Father to have all those mysterious cupboards opened, whose hinges could be seen high up in the wall; he laughed at us and asked how even an ugly dwarf could jump so high and disappear in an instant through tightly fastened panels. It was all very fine laughing, we children said, but it was most certain that the ogre had his home there; and in future we had to go on living in the same house with a nasty little dwarf, just because he could jump high. How the younger children in their fright would scuttle past that Blue Room door, even in the daytime!"

I only hope the ghost will leave the present occupants in peace.

Yours faithfully,
Mary Petre.

Tor Bryan, Ingatestone, Essex.

A highly interesting account concerning what may well be one of the last authentic Essex witches, is given me by Mrs. N. S. Mungo Park, of Stomps, Great Canfield, Dunmow. She says that the Reverend Mr. Vincent, who was Vicar of High Easter, told her that an old man of the village, referring to a certain woman in the parish who was credited with being a witch, told the following story, which I give in Mrs. Mungo Park's own words:

It appeared that a girl in the village had something very wrong with one of her legs, and a "wise woman" whom she had consulted told her that she had been "overlooked" by the witch— but she could be cured. Her mother was to light the copper, get the water nearly boiling and seat the girl on the edge of the copper with her bad leg in the hot water, and to keep it in as long as she could bear it. Afterwards she was to be put to bed. This was done and next morning the leg was healed.

"Now," said the wise woman; "go you to the witch's cottage, and you will see what you will see!" What they *did* see was that the witch's leg was scalded and burnt from the knee to the ankle.

Another of the old man's anecdotes was of a child who was sent on a message to a cottage. On her return she said to her mother, "That's a strange place! I saw the cat and the meece [mice] eating from the same dish."

"Never you go there again," said her mother. "Where the cat and the meece eat from the same dish the woman is *always* a witch."

Mrs. Mungo Park adds, dryly, "I have three cats and I frequently tell them this story, hoping that it will penetrate!" She tells me that the last witch to be ducked in England, was ducked in the Doctor's Pond at Dunmow, in 1882.

An amusing but far from edifying witch story is sent me by my good old friend Mr. T. W. Morley, of Holywell Row, on the Suffolk edge of the fens. Mr. Morley is a true East Anglian villager, and after a lifetime spent as a builder on farms and amid the Brecks and the wild fen, he is a fount of rural lore and local superstitions.

Writing to me he says:

Between 1906 and 1912 I was working at Herringswell Manor, near Newmarket. The Head Keeper, Mr Edgar Sparkes, an old friend of mine and a man not given to telling frivolous tales, told me in all seriousness that as a lad he was riding to Bury St. Edmunds in their pony trap, when they passed a queer looking old lady who said: "Give us a lift, Guv'nor." His father took one look at her and refused. She replied: "You will remember me before you get home." And he did. In his own words he was "lousy from head to foot and every bit of clothing had to be burnt!"

Mr. Morley sheds new light on the old legend of the ghostly maiden who was said to haunt the now-demolished old Manor House at Mildenhall in Suffolk, for long the seat of the Bunburys.

I was working in about 1901 on the reconstruction of a sitting room [he writes] when one of the men, excavating under the floor came across some bones. They were carefully collected and after being examined by an expert, were said to be those of a young female, and taken away and interred elsewhere. An old servant in the house told me quietly: "This is the room where Colonel North murdered his daughter and buried her under the floor."

About thirty years afterwards, I was working on Ampton Church, when I lifted a section of the floor and under it found a small crypt containing in lead caskets the bodies of a Colonel North and of a young woman. I could not help wondering if the unfortunate girl was really in her casket, or whether it was empty.

Legends of imps, the familiars of witches, are common enough in various parts of East Anglia, particularly in Essex, but Mr. Morley tells me of a new and hitherto unrecorded nest of imps. Years ago, he met an old man with white hair and a long white beard who said to him; "You remind me of a lad I used to know in Swaffham Prior in Cambridgeshire. There was an old woman there that we were both afraid of. She used to ask us to go to the shop for her and we daren't refuse. One day she gave us both a piece of cake, and leaving us sitting in her cottage parlour, went out to get some potatoes, saying as she left the room: 'Don't you dare touch that box.' The moment she was gone the other boy lifted the lid and we got a glimpse of a horrible, crawling, rolling mass of awful-looking creatures with queer heads, squeaking as they rolled over one another. We had only time to get a glimpse of them before the old lady was back into the room like a shot and let out a fearful yell. We lit out of that cottage as fast as we could go! We were told afterwards that she was a witch and that these were her imps."

Not long after [says Mr. Morley] I had an assistant from Swaffham Prior, who told me that one of the villagers reported seeing something in white sitting in a ploughed field at night. He rushed into the pub and told the locals. They laughed at him. So, just before closing time, he left the pub, wrapped himself in a sheet and sat at the end of the ploughed field just as the chaps were turning out of the pub. As they approached him he turned his head *and saw something in white sitting in the ploughed field just behind him!* He was out of that field like a shot and legged it for home as fast as he could go.

Mr. Morley records that when he was a boy, an old woman called Mrs. Eley in his native village, reputed to be a witch, lived in a cottage with her daughter Maria, and a black and white cat. The daughter was one-armed, as the witch was said to have chopped the other arm off when the girl became engaged to a young man of whom she did not approve.

Mr. Morley says that he and other boys were so terrified of the cat which had a sinister habit of turning up in the most unexpected places, that they ambushed it one day, pelted it with stones, but failed to hit it. When they returned to the village they found the old witch in a rage, and, says Mr. Morley: "She cursed us and threatened that if we ever touched her cat she would turn us all into animals and nobody would ever know us. She was gaunt and bent and walked with a crutch, and her face was thin and yellow and so evil that she frightened the life out of us."

This indefatigable story-teller of the Fenland, who has

gone to immense pains to provide me with village beliefs and
legends for this book says, in a further letter, written in 1953:

When I was a boy I had to come from Beck Row to Holywell
Row weekly to collect the butter—10d. to 1/-d. a pound then—
and I had to pass Whitings Farm which was said to be haunted.
It stood empty for several years, and I think there must be something sinister about it, as two men have committed suicide there
in my time. On my way home I had to pass Aspal Hall and Beck
Lodge and the horsekeeper told me when he has been going home
late on different occasions he has seen a lady in a long, black
cloak pass along the road and right through a bricked-up gateway
in the wall. I did not loiter here at night, and heaved a sigh of
relief when I passed that door!

Another old friend of mine, a man I greatly respected, told me
he and some friends were passing Aspal Farm one night when
something huge passed them, shaking the ground as it went, and
saying: "Don't fear me—fear my follower." Immediately something passed them like a terrific gust of wind, but nothing was
seen. The farm where his parents lived, also had a bad reputation.
When they got to bed at night, sometimes all the bells would start
ringing, for no apparent reason. As this happened too often, the
bells were taken out. At other times they would hear the crockery
being smashed, but nothing was found even broken.

Another very old friend with whom I fished for many years,
lived in West Row. He told me there was a hare in a certain field
that none of their dogs could catch. As it always went the same
way they decided to catch it by some other means so they put their
dogs in the field and, of course, the hare made off the same way
as usual, but a Mr. Boyce was waiting at the other end of the field
with his gun. He promptly shot the hare, which uttered a piercing,
unearthly scream. At the same time an old lady named Mrs.
Jerrington was burned to death in her chair. She was said to have
been the hare.

Here is one told me by my grandmother. A smallholder in
Lakenheath could not get any butter from his milk. After continuous churning, and no results, he came to the conclusion the cows
were bewitched, and blamed an old lady living nearby. Someone
stole some of the old lady's hair. This was put on the fire and

burnt. At the same time some of the milk was brought to a boil. All the doors and windows were securely fastened and everyone had orders to be perfectly quiet. As the milk boiled and the hair burned, up came the old woman on her broom, or whatever conveyance she used, shouting, "Let me in. Let me in." Someone said "Listen" and the spell was broken, otherwise her leg would have burst and the milk become normal again.

My father told me another story, this was of an old man living in Lakenheath who was very miserly and very mean. One day he was found at the bottom of the staircase with his neck broken. It was thought he had fallen downstairs, but it was found out afterwards that a poor old lady had called there begging, but he had refused to help her, and slammed the door in her face. When the door was open one day, a cat crept in, which the old man could not get rid of. When he went to bed, it was waiting upstairs in the form of a witch, and pushed him downstairs, backwards.

An old friend of mine, still living in Mildenhall, rented a house on Whitehouse Drove on the Mildenhall-Littleport road, near the Little Ouse river.

The former tenant told him, "You won't be there long", and when my friend asked him why, he said, "You will soon find out." "And," said my friend, "I did. There were such unearthly noises at night, we were unable to sleep." He told his wife it was the horses in the meadow, but said he knew different. Sometimes it sounded like someone rending up the floors, and it got so bad his wife would not be left there alone, so in the end they left it as soon as they could. I don't think anyone lived there afterwards, and I believe the house was eventually pulled down. The fenman, being a rather reserved sort of person, talks very little about these things for fear of being laughed at.

Another remarkable story from the fens was sent to me by Mr. William Markall, of Longstone Crescent, Frecheville, Sheffield, who writes:

My mother and her parents lived in the house next to Southery old Churchyard. A friend of the family set out one misty morning for Littleport, with horse and trap. The horse was blind, and instead of taking the turning to the bridge it turned into the river, and horse and occupants of the trap were drowned. My mother, a girl at the time, woke in the morning of that same day to see the figure of the old lady leaning over the foot of her bed; and her father, also in the same morning, going to work saw the figure of the old lady hurrying along the path in front of him. He called without receiving an answer. . . .

That is all. I hope your reception of this perfectly true story—which may be verified by a report of the accident in the local paper of the day, somewhere about 1875—will be like my own, which is to welcome something not legend, not invention, but of truly scientific interest, however lacking in meaning or moral.

Mr. Maurice Mottram, of Three Owls, Holt Road, Cromer, a cousin of my old friend Mr. R. H. Mottram, the distinguished novelist, has a delicious Norfolk legend to the effect that there was a local belief that the Ark came to rest on Mulbarton Common.

An old inhabitant repeated this to a stranger who expressed some doubt as to the correctness of this. The old inhabitant, who probably knew little of the world beyond what he could see, and was correspondingly parochial in his outlook replied with some heat: "That must be true. Where else could it ha' grounded? Aren't this the highest bit o' ground for miles round?"

The story goes on:

When ole Nick see tha Ark he got inter a poont (punt) an' curled his tail up under the thwart and come rowing around just as Noah had opened the winder to let the dove in. And Nick sings out: "Mornin' Cap'n Noah. Nice mornin' arter the rain." But ole Noah he see Nick's tail a-curled up under the thwart an' he sings out: "You go to Hell" and bangs the winder down!

Another Norfolk superstition sent me by Colonel S. E. Glendenning, D.S.O., F.S.A., of Rosary Road, Thorpe Hamlet, Norwich, is to the effect that the devil gets into blackberries on November 1st and, says Colonel Glendenning: "My mother, born over 100 years ago, got the yarn either in the Ormesby or the Ranworth district. She was a highly educated lady and did not think the Devil was concerned, but was obviously worried when I told her I had found some ripe blackberries in the first week in November. 'You shouldn't have eaten them. There is something wrong with them after November 1st.' I agree they are not very nice as late as this, but I hardly think this accounts for the superstition."

Ghostly coaches are familiar apparitions in most counties, but although I have known that charming Norfolk village of Weybourne and the bleak enchanted marshes of Salthouse for many years, I confess that the story sent me by Mrs. Iris Brayne, a holder of the Kaiser I Hind Medal, of The Glebe, Ashill near Thetford, is new to me. Mrs Brayne writes:

> When I was a little girl (and I am now an old woman) my great-uncle owned a large portion of Weybourne and cultivated the Home Farm himself. One evening when I was staying there the team-man came in trembling with fright and told how, as he was bringing his horses home, a coach and four had come galloping down the street and the driver was without a head, and they had all disappeared through the churchyard wall. I went with him and saw his terrified horses. My great-uncle, William Bolding, then told me that this ghost had been seen several times before.
>
> He also told me about a blue sow who used to cross the road between Kelling and Salthouse and no hedge would grow there, but that one amused him, as he thought it was like some holes in his hedges where the smugglers crossed his land. He said that every now and then a keg of brandy or some silk would be left in his porch because he did not report them or worry them! I still have a silk sash that he found on his doorstep long ago and gave to me when I was a little girl.

On that bleak coast to the south there stands, with its face to the sandhills and its back to the reedy wastes and gleaming waters of Hickling Broad and the Brograve Level, the old

Hall of Waxham. A bleakly beautiful little manor-house set behind an embattled wall, with a great gaunt church and a mighty flint-built barn to keep it company. Half the ancient lands of Waxham lie under the sea, and the Hall itself is said to be haunted by the unshriven spirits of the Brograves who died violently. First, Sir Ralph who died in the Crusades on a Saracen's spear, then Sir Edmund who fell in the Barons' Wars. Sir John was killed by an arrow at Agincourt and Sir Francis in the Wars of the Roses, fighting for the Lancastrians. Sir Thomas was slain at Marston Moor and Sir Charles fell at Ramillies under Marlborough.

Sir Barney died a bachelor, although he dotted the countryside with his portrait. On New Year's Eve he gave a banquet to the shades of his departed ancestors, when covers, and nothing else, were laid for the six ghostly visitants. The seventh was more substantially supplied. Glasses were filled for each guest and their toasts solemnly drunk. At midnight the wraiths vanished and later Sir Barney awoke, tired, cold, and with a hangover.

His fights and bets were fantastic. When a sweep overcharged him for cleaning the Hall chimneys, he fought the man but got the worst of it because he knocked so much soot out of the sweep's clothes that it nearly choked him. It took a week's hard drinking to remove the taste of it.

The late Walter Rye had an enchanting tale of a local marshman's verdict on Sir Barney in these words:

[1]Owd Sir Barney Brograve he wur a werry bad old man and he sold his soul to the Devil and guv him a parchment bond. When he died he went and called on the Devil and say to him "Here I be" and the Devil he say; "Sir Barney, I allus sed you was a perfect gentleman"—and Sir Barney he say; "Well, you might ask me to set down" but the Devil he say; "I've been looking trew your account and it fare to me if I hev you in here 'twon't be a sennight afore yew'll be top-dog and I shall hev to play second

[1] *Norfolk and Norwich Notes and Queries*, January 27th, 1906.

137

fiddle, so there's your writing back, and now be off!" And Sir Barney, he say; "Where am I to go tew?" and the owd Devil he forgot hisself and got angry and he say; "Go to hell!" Sir Barney he had no idea of wandering all about nowhere, so he tuk him at his word and he sat down and stayed. And they du say there's tew Devils there now.

Binham, five miles south-east of Wells-next-the-Sea, possesses the beautiful remains of a Benedictine Priory, about which they tell the grim legend of a fiddler and his dog, lost in an underground tunnel. Oddly enough, when the County Council workmen were excavating at a place called Fiddler's Hill, about two miles away in April 1935, they discovered the skeletons of a man and a dog, which I understand, were verified by Dr. Hicks of Wells-next-the-Sea.

The original story was beautifully told in dialect in *The East Anglian Hand-book* in 1892, and that version I give here. It will be noted, however, that according to the dialect story-teller, the dog returned above ground, but his master was never seen again. This does not agree with the account of the finding of the bones in 1935. However, here is the tale as it was told in the true Norfolk tongue in 1892.

"So you want to go to Binham, eh, sir? Ah, them there old abbeys are funny places and there's funny tales told about 'em. Some on 'em true, tu, as I know well, sir. I s'pose you ha' bin to Walsin'ham?"

I nodded, and the old man went on: "Walsin'ham was the finest place of the two, I'm told, though Binham had a name er its own. Do you know, sir, there's a subt'tanim passage atween them two right underground. You can see it as you goo along the road, runnin' across the medders like a grate green bank and I ha' sin 'em a-borin' down to try an' find out mor about it—specially where it cross the road and where you can hear the holler sound on't as you drive over it. Them old monks used to be up to curis [curious] kind o' games, and I 'spect that when they got kinder tired o' their own company they used to goo tru this underground passage to see the folks at the other end. Went a-wisitin' yer know, sir.

138

Sir Barney Brograve and the Devil

"Thare are folks who say that once was ther time that every night a grate tall feller, like an old monk, and dressed in black, used to walk along on top o' the bank right from Walsin'ham to Binham, shakin' his ugly owd hid and 'pearin' just as if he was a-lookin' fer suffin' he could never find. I ha' never sin him, but my grandsir hev many a time, though none ever clapped eyes on him sin the fiddler went down thare and never cum back.

"Yer see, sir, once was the time that sum of the bank, close to the abbey, kinder caved in, and a lot on 'em went to see it and to peep into the dark old passage. They daren't goo in, or at least, not for far, but while they were a-poakin' and a-paarin' who should come up but old Jimmy Griggs the fiddler. Jimmy was afeared o' naught and he sa'; 'Clear away, together, I'm a-goin' in,' and in he went and his dog Trap with him.

"Jimmy had his fiddle with him, and he sa'; 'I'll keep on a-playin' and yow together goo along the top o' the bank and then yow'll know whare I am.' An', so they did an' they haard him a-playin' under the ground, just one tune and then another. All er a sudden the tune stopped and they couldn't haar anything. They called and shouted but, sir, my grandsir said as how there wor never a sound.

"Sum said one thing and sum said another, but while they were a-considerin' what tu du, one on 'em sa'; 'Why if here ain't old Trap' and thare was the dog beside 'em sure enuff, with his tail atween his legs and a-shiverin' as if he wor mortal skeered.

"They went back to the hole, sir, and peeped in but it wor dark as the grave and jest as quiet. They never saw Jimmy any more, and in the night thare was a storm such as they had never known afore, and when mornin' came that place whare he went in was all broken down 'er haap and folks told the tale far and wide that Jimmy Griggs the fiddler had been carried off by the Black Monk.

"Yes, sir, I s'pose they ought to ha' sarched further, but they didn't and poor old Griggs had ne'er a friend to trouble arter him and we haard no more about it. But ever sin' then they ha' called that bank 'Fiddler's Hill'."

Between Wells and Blakeney lies the tiny coastal village of Wiveton, with a small but really lovely Elizabethan Hall. Of this house, the issue of *Norfolk and Norwich Notes and*

Queries for February 3rd, 1900, had a highly interesting story to tell which was quoted from an unnamed American newspaper of some date presumably of that period. The story was as follows:

> In one of the least known villages on the Norfolk coast, a place called Wiveton, is an Elizabethan house named Wiveton Hall. It is in a fine state of preservation and looks quite likely to last another three centuries, in spite of the terrific gales which vent their full rage on its exposed and weather-beaten walls.
>
> In this ancient house, some years since, was discovered a door, heavily plated with iron, giving access to some room which had been closed and unentered for probably half a century. The former occupants of the place seem to have felt no particular interest as to what might be behind this mysterious door and so left it undisturbed. On the house changing hands, the new proprietor was of a more curious disposition and determined to have the door opened. The iron plates were cut through and after considerable trouble access was obtained to the chamber. It proved to be absolutely empty and the floor had entirely rotted away.
>
> On one of the walls, however, was the impress of a hand made with some dark pigment, giving the idea that someone had smeared his hand with it and then pressed it on the wall, palm downwards. This pigment was said to have been human blood, but as to the truth of this we cannot say. One can only wonder what dark tragedy this room, so long untenanted, may hide.

If you go south by east of Wiveton along the coast, you come to the bleakly beautiful and windy little village of Hasbro', famous for its lighthouse and its wrecks. At Hasbro', which the maps and guide-books spell Happisburgh, they have a remarkable ghost story, well told by the late E. R. Suffling many years ago, in his *History and Legends of the Broads District*.

The story, according to Suffling, who was writing at the end of the last century, centres on Pump Hill. He says:

> When the following incidents occurred I cannot exactly say, but from all accounts it must have been at the beginning of the present

century, when a good business was done in this village in the landing of silk, lace, tobacco, spirits, etc., under cover of night and a sovereign to cover each eye of the authorities.

It appears that farmers coming home late at night were sometimes terribly frightened at a figure they saw coming up the main street of the village from the direction of the Cart Gap. It was an unusual figure, even for a ghost, for although it made good progress, it was legless and, I might add, headless, for its head hung down its back between the shoulders. In its arms it carried a long bundle, but what the package contained none knew, not even those who had seen it.

It was evidently a sailor, for it was dressed in the petticoat-looking garment in vogue among sea-faring men in those days, moreover it wore a broad leathern belt with a huge brass buckle, in which was thrust a pistol and a long pig-tail graced its head, it nearly trailed the ground.

After several farmers had been frightened nearly out of their lives by this legless mariner, two of them, more hardy than the rest, resolved to watch his ghostship. Several nights they watched vainly, but at last one night came the bold smuggler sure enough and the farmers quakingly followed it. Although its head was reversed and turned away from the direction in which it was going, it still kept a straight course along the middle of the road until it came to the well; here it paused and balancing its burden in its arms, dropped it endways down the mouth and after gliding aimlessly around for a minute or so, quietly disappeared down the well also.

The farmers' story was next day told at a village council and by many heartily laughed at. . . . At length it was agreed to search the Well, so ropes and ladders, etc., being procured, a volunteer was quickly found to make the descent. A lighted candle was first lowered in a ball of clay to test the atmosphere, which being found pure, a looped rope, in which a young man was seated, was carefully lowered.

Forty feet he went down with a lantern but could see nothing, and was being hauled up again when he caught sight of a piece of dark blue cloth hanging on a projecting brick. This was exhibited and again young Harmer descended, this time armed with a long clothes prop. Anxious moments followed and then came his voice up the well-shaft in strange sepulchral tones "I can feel something soft at the bottom."

Accordingly an iron hake (pot-hook) tied to a clothes line was lowered to him, and after a while he succeeded in entangling it in something. He was hauled up and then the clothes line too, and at the end of it came up a sodden sack tied at the mouth. It was eagerly opened and a pair of boots protruded, which upon being withdrawn were found to contain the legs of their owner hacked off at the thighs.

Harmer was asked to try his luck down the Well once more, but he declined to venture, his find having shaken his nerves very considerably. With the help of a little Dutch courage a fisherman was at length prevailed upon to go down and see what he could grapple. Down he went and those who could crowd near enough to the Well-side to peer down, saw him at work angling with his line and hake; but a long time went by without any result. Something soft he could feel with the clothes prop, but he could not hook it; he wanted more refreshment, so a bottle of rum and water, attached to a string, was lowered to him.

After a refresher he again went to work, and presently hooked a weighty object and gave the signal to haul him up; just as they were doing this, the "object" was hauled from the water by those in charge of the clothes line, putting his light out. However, the villagers hauled at both ropes and the fisherman quickly appeared, bearing in his arms, or rather half-supporting, a huge mass of what looked like wet clothing.

Quickly dropping it on the ground upon arriving on terra firma, he turned it over and to the horror of those present, revealed to view the decomposed body of a man, whose head was only attached to the body by a small flap at the back of the neck. There was the broad leathern belt with a pistol still hanging in it, and the peculiar petticoat of the period; in fact everything just as the farmers had described as appertaining to the ghost.

Search was made and in a week or so, evidence was brought to show that the black-bearded sailor had been murdered near the Cart Gap, as a large patch of blood and the corresponding pistol to that in his belt, was found in a desolate bullock-shed close by. Three or four gold pieces were also found embedded in the earth and fragments of three empty Schiedam bottles were strewn about. Nothing was ever discovered of the murderers, nor was it ever heard who the murdered man was.

It was at the time supposed that there had been a row among some smugglers and that in dividing their spoil one of them had quarrelled with his comrades, who had killed him by nearly severing his head from his body, and that to make the corpse easier of carriage to the Well, they had hacked off his legs and placed them in the sack in which they were found. The money trodden into the soil gives colour to the theory of the division of the spoil and the broken bottles (three) shows there must have been several carousers.

Not far from Hasbro' is Bacton, haunted by "The Long Coastguardsman". He walks to Mundesley on dark nights as the clock strikes twelve. He loves storms and gales, when he sings and shouts at the top of his voice. If there is a lull in the shrieking of the wind, he laughs loudly, whilst at other times his cries for help can be heard from far off. No one knows who he is. Few people have heard him. But everyone knows someone who has.

Probably the best known and certainly the best authenticated Norfolk ghost story is that of the ghost of Mannington Hall, a lovely old fifteenth-century moated mansion about two miles from Corpusty, for long the property of the Walpoles and tenanted for some years by a friend of my own, who certainly did not deny the story to me.

The Mannington ghost has been written of at various times, sometimes in garbled fashion, but I think there can be no doubt of the sober authenticity of the account given in the eighties by the late Dr. Augustus Jessop, the well-known antiquary, who distinctly saw the ghost while staying at the Hall.

His account of it appeared in the *Athenaeum* of January 1880, and is as follows:

On the 10th of October, 1879, Dr. Jessop drove to Lord Orford's from Norwich. It was his intention to spend some time at the Hall in examining and making extracts from various scarce works which he had long been seeking for, and which he now learnt were in Lord Orford's library. He arrived at Mannington at four in the afternoon, and, after some agreeable conversation, dressed for dinner. Dinner took place at seven, and was partaken of by six persons, including Dr. Jessop and his host. The conversation is declared to have been of a pleasant character, to have been chiefly concerned with artistic questions, and the experiences of men of the world, and to have never trenched upon supernatural subjects.

After dinner cards were introduced, and at half-past ten, two of the guests having to leave, the party broke up. Dr. Jessop now desired to be permitted to sit up for some hours in order to make extracts from the works already referred to. Lord Orford wished to leave a valet with his guest, but the Doctor, deeming that this might embarrass him, and cause him to go to bed earlier than he wished, requested to be left alone. This was agreed to, the servants were dismissed and his host and his other guests retired to their rooms, so that by eleven o'clock Dr. Jessop was the only person downstairs.

The apartment in which he was preparing to set to work for a few hours is a large one with a huge fire-place and a great old-fashioned chimney, and is furnished with every luxury. The library, whence Dr. Jessop had to bring such volumes as he needed opens into this room, and in order to obtain the works he wanted he had not only to go into it, but when there, to mount a chair, to get down the book he required.

In his very circumstantial account of the affair the antiquary relates that he had altogether six small volumes, which he took down from their shelves and placed in a little pile on the table at his right hand. In a little while he was busily at work. Sometimes reading, sometimes writing, and thoroughly absorbed in his occupation. As he finished with a book, he placed it in front of him, and then proceeded with the next, and so on until he had only one volume of his little pile of tomes left to deal with.

The antiquary, being as he states, of a chilly temperament, sat himself at a corner of the table with the fire-place at his left. Occasionally he rose, knocked the fire together, and stood up to warm his feet. In this manner he went on until nearly 1 o'clock, when he appears to have congratulated himself upon the rapid progress he had made with his task, and that after all he should get to bed by two. He got up and wound his watch, opened a bottle of seltzer water, and then, re-seating himself at the table, upon which were four silver candlesticks containing lighted candles, he set to work upon the last little book of the heap.

What now happened must be told in Dr. Jessop's own words: "I had been engaged upon it about half an hour [referring to the volume] and was just beginning to think that my work was drawing to a close, when, as I was actually writing, I saw a large white hand within a foot of my elbow.

"Turning my head, there sat a figure of a somewhat large man, with his back to the fire, bending slightly over the table, and apparently examining the pile of books I had been engaged upon. The man's face was turned away from me, but I saw his closely-cut, reddish-brown hair, his ear and shaved cheek, the eyebrows, the corner of the right eye, the side of the forehead and the large high cheek bone.

"He was dressed in what I can only describe as a kind of ecclesiastical habit of corded silk, close up to the throat, with a narrow rim of edging of about an inch broad of satin or velvet serving as a stand-up collar and fitting close to the chin. The right hand, which had first attracted my attention, was clasping without any great pressure the left hand; both hands were in perfect repose, and the large, blue veins of the right hand were conspicuous. I remember thinking that the hand was like the hand of Velasquez's magnificent "Dead Knight" in the National Gallery.

"I looked at my visitor for some seconds, and was perfectly sure that he was not a reality. A thousand thoughts came crowding upon me, but not the least feeling of alarm or even uneasiness; curiosity and a strong interest were uppermost. For an instant I felt eager to make a sketch of my friend, and I looked at a tray on my right for a pencil; then I thought, 'Upstairs I have a sketch book; shall I fetch it?'

"There he sat, and I was fascinated—afraid, not of his staying, but lest he should go. Stopping in my writing, I lifted my left hand from the paper, stretched it out to the pile of books, and moved the top one. I cannot explain why I did this—my arm passed in front of the figure, and it vanished.

"I was simply disappointed, and nothing more. I went on with

147

my writing as if nothing had happened, perhaps for another five minutes, and had actually got to the last few words of what I had determined to extract, when the figure appeared again, exactly in the same place and attitude as before.

"I saw the hands close to my own; I turned my head again to examine him more closely, and I was framing a sentence to address him, when I discovered that I dare not speak; I was afraid of the sound of my own voice. There he sat, and there sat I. I turned my head again to my work, and finished writing the two or three words I still had to write. The paper and my notes are at this moment before me and exhibit not the slightest tremor or nervousness. I could point out the words I was writing when the phantom came and when he disappeared.

"Having finished my task, I shut the book and threw it on the table. It made a slight noise as it fell, and the figure vanished.

"Throwing myself back in my chair, I sat for some seconds looking at the fire with a curious mixture of feeling, and I remember wondering whether my friend would come again, and, if he did, whether he would hide the fire from me. Then first there stole upon me a dread and a suspicion that I was beginning to lose my nerve. I remember yawning; then I rose and lit my bedroom candle, took my books into the inner library, mounted the chair as before, and replaced five of the volumes; the sixth I brought back, and laid it upon the table where I had been writing, when the phantom did me the honour to appear to me.

"By this time I had lost all sense of uneasiness. I blew out all the candles and marched off to bed, where I slept the sleep of the just—or the guilty, I know not which, but I slept very soundly. And that is the conclusion of the story; but whether hallucination, spectral illusion, or trickery, no one has been enabled to prove, and as the hero of the tale declines to proffer explanation, theory, or inference, the affair continues to be a mystery."

An equally famous Norfolk ghost, by no means so well-authenticated, is the Brown Lady of Raynham Hall, the seat of the Marquess Townshend. Lady Dorothy Nevill, in her book, *Mannington and the Walpoles,* calls her "the ill-fated Dorothy, who married Charles, second Viscount

Townshend and who died tragically by falling down the grand staircase and became the terror of the visitors and servants at Raynham".

But the contemporary announcement of her death fixes the date as March 29th, 1726, and says she died of smallpox.

When the Townshend heirlooms were sold at Christies in March 1904, her portrait was described as "The Brown Lady. Dorothy Walpole, wife of the second and most famous Marquess Townshend." She is said to have been a young and beautiful girl forced to marry an old man against her will; but Peter Wentworth, writing to Lady Strafford on February 20th, 1713, says: "Here is an extraordinary wedding a going to be—Lord Tounsend to Dolly Walpole— I can't tell you whether you know her carrecter but she is won [one] Lord Wharton 'kept'."

The late Walter Rye, who knew more about Norfolk history than most people, said that she was supposed to haunt the State Bedroom, where she frightened George IV, when Prince Regent, out of his wits. He reported that he saw "a little lady all dressed in brown with dishevelled hair and a face of ashy paleness" by his bedside and "with many oaths" said; "I will not pass another hour in this accursed house, for I have seen that what I hope to God I may never see again."

Walter Rye then says: "It is a pity to have to disbelieve the story told so minutely—how the Brown Lady had been seen by the servants and was waited up for by the gentlemen—how they stayed two nights in the corridor playing ecarté, with two game-keepers at each door—how they saw nothing the first two nights but that in the middle of the third, one of the keepers called out 'There she be' and they saw her come through the wall at them—how one gentleman most wisely flattened himself against the wall, to get as far as possible from her, but the other boldly stretching out his arms till he touched either side of the corridor was passed through by her like smoke is passed through, and how they both saw her disappear through another wall."

What would seem to be the best summing-up of this much-disputed story, was given in the *East Anglian Hand-book* in June 1885, which printed the following:

> Lady Dorothy Townshend, whom tradition still credits with haunting the staircase of Raynham Hall, was the daughter of Robert Walpole of Houghton, to whose care the young Viscount Townshend had been entrusted. Young Townshend conceived an ardent affection for his guardian's daughter, but his suit was refused by her father on the ground that suspicion would be attached to himself of compassing a match so advantageous to himself and family by improper means. Dorothy was then scarce fifteen. Lord Townshend twelve years older and he, obeying his guardian's monition, married another lady in 1699.
>
> After her death, however, he returned to his first love, and was united to Dorothy Walpole in the July of 1713, she being then in her twenty-sixth year. According to the legend an estrangement took place between them, the wife was kept straitly within her own apartments and harshly, if not cruelly, treated by her husband, till on March 29th, 1726, she died of a broken heart, since which time she has from time to time traversed in ghostly guise the scenes of her mortal sufferings, haunting especially the oaken staircase of Raynham Hall.
>
> But truth, historical truth, is totally at variance with the legend. She really died of smallpox on the date named, but regretted and lamented by all who knew her, specially so by her husband, whose grief was most intense. She died in the 40th year of her age, generally and justly lamented for her uncommon merit and the accomplishments of her mind as well as of her person. Lord Townshend, after resigning the post he held under the Government, passed the remainder of his life in seclusion.

Wolterton Hall, not far from Mannington, is the present seat of Lord Walpole. It was badly damaged by fire early in 1953, but Lord Walpole tells me that he intends to restore it. This house, a superb example of its period, is supposed to be haunted by a White Lady. According to Lady Dorothy Nevill, Ambassador Horace Walpole married a Miss Lombard. A large Conversation Piece was painted, comprising the Ambassador and his wife and seven or eight children, some of them represented as angels, since they apparently died as babies. Lady Dorothy's father cut this picture up and gave the portrait to different members of the family, the descendants of the original figures in the Conversation Piece, and according to Lady Dorothy: "The unhappy wife, Miss Lombard, is said to haunt Wolterton seeking for her divided relatives."

She goes on to say:

For many years Wolterton was abandoned as a residence and left to desolation and decay; but shortly after my nephew, the present Lord Orford, succeeded to the estate, he decided to return to the home of his ancestors, and during the last few years has done everything in his power to restore the house to its old state and replace as many of the contents as can be gathered together —a difficult task, in which, however, owing to untiring effort, he has been extremely successful. . . .

There was at Wolterton a Nelson room, in which the great Admiral had slept on a visit. Nelson's picture—a personal gift— painted by Lane, is now, unfortunately, lost to us for ever, for it was burnt in the great fire at the Pantechnicon, where it had been deposited for safe keeping. . . . My father was very fond of birds and the lawns and pastures used to be enlivened by the presence of golden pheasants and other feathered pets of brilliant plumage. Now once again these lawns and walks, where I played as a child, are resuming something of their old appearance, after forty years of neglect and destruction; my nephew, the present Lord Orford, as I have before said, having piously devoted much time, thought and money to restoring the home of his forefathers to its original state.

There is a family ghost at Wolterton, which at intervals is seen by old servants about the place. A White Lady is said to be in the habit of appearing whenever some calamity is about to threaten our family. Some little time before my brother, the late Lord

Orford, died in 1894, I well recollect his saying to me, "I hear from Norfolk that the White Lady has been seen again. It is you or I this time, Dolly, for we are the only ones left."

The White Lady in question is supposed to be one of the Scamler family, who were the possessors of Wolterton before my ancestor built the present mansion. There used to be some story that one of the Lords Orford unearthed the old tombstones of the Scamlers in the ruined church in Wolterton Park, and that this act of sacrilege was the cause of the poor lady's spirit being so disturbed. But I have recently discovered that no act of this kind was ever perpetrated at all, so it must be for some other reason that the ghostly dame lingers about Wolterton. In old days the Walpoles used to be driven in their hearse three times around this ruined church before being laid to rest in the family vault. Certainly Lady Walpole of Wolterton (Pierre Lombard's daughter) was buried with this ceremonial.

CHAPTER IX

On Wills-o'-the-Wisp and Corpse Candles

WHEN the fen farmer of pre-1914 days rattled home from market in spring cart or high-wheeled gig, he drove to his lonely thatched homestead over soft and peaty roads, where wheels sank deep and shockheaded willows edged bottomless dykes, shining dully in the moon. A flat and misty land where plover wailed, cattle snuffled in the fog, and on nights of spring, the deep and ghostly boom of the bittern sounded hollow in the dark.

Often have I heard that muffled, thudding "oomp-oomp-br'oomp!" which is like no other sound on earth. That, alone, is enough to chill the blood of any man unaccustomed to it who finds himself on a dark night in a dark world of whispering reeds and wailing peewits, of owls, and sheep that cough in the mist, like men whose throats have been cut.

Imagine, then, the terror of the Fenman homing down a lonely "drove" through such a wild and manless marshland world, when he sees, flitting over the bogs and stinking pools, a lambent yellow flame, like a candle in a horn lantern, bobbing up and down, as one said to me "like a hoppity little owd man wi' a wooden leg".

If this midnight light of mystery, the dreaded Will-o'-the-Wisp or Jack-o'-Lantern, came bobbing along the rough fen drove, it was ten to one that the farmer's horse would shy and tip the cart into the dyke. If the man was on foot, he ran for his life, or, if of sterner or more inquisitive stuff, followed the Will, only to land up to his neck in some rotten swamp which closed over him.

Small wonder then, that the fear of the Will, sometimes called Hob-o'-Lantern or the Lantern Man—in Swaffham Fen, in Cambridgeshire, they are known as Jenny-Burnt-Arses—is still a rooted belief in all marshland areas. The Will was, in reality, no more than a spontaneous combustion of marsh gas which occurred on warm nights in rotten bogs and deep fen pools, but with the increased drainage of Fens and marshes, the Will is now almost unknown.

I am told that they still occur on certain bogs in West Wales and it would never surprise me to see one on a hot summer night round Barton Broad, on the swamps that lie between Hickling and Horsey, on the Martham Marshes, about Upton Broad or, for that matter, in half a dozen other places in Broadland.

They were spoken of as commonplace and comparatively recent occurrences in Wicken and Burwell Fens in Cambridgeshire when I was a boy. I remember, in about 1910, a horseman, employed by the father of my old school friend, Group-Captain Donald Fleming, D.F.C., who then lived at Henny Hill Farm, near Soham, fired his gun at one one night and then bolted. The Norfolk Broads district, the Fens, the North Kent Marshes and many of the Welsh marsh districts, are full of tales of Wills.

Mrs. Hilda M. Brown, of West Winds, Catherine Road, Woodbridge, Suffolk, whose father was a well-known yeoman farmer in the Cambridgeshire Fens, tells me that, in her youth, coming home one summer night between Whittlesey and Standground, only three miles from the centre of Peter-borough "one rose up out of a swamp just at the bottom of the bank I was walking along. I went down to get a closer view of it, when it immediately danced away across the fields. That was the closest I have ever been to one.

"My mother was awakened too, one night, by one shining on the bedroom window, and as she watched it, it seemed to rise up too and flit away across the fields. It was a very bright one. My grandfather, a Lincolnshire farmer and a centenarian, used to say that when they were seen, it was a sign of rain very soon.

"Some years ago the *Peterborough Advertiser* printed an article by W.H.B.S., in which it stated: 'The favourite haunts were Chatteris, Whittlesey, Peterborough, and Thorney, but after Turf Fen was drained at Chatteris, they were rarely seen afterwards in that district.' In some districts," Mrs. Brown goes on, "they were red in colour, and others like an ordinary candle in colour. The late Mr. T. W. Holditch, of Peterborough, referred to them as Corpse Candles, and there was an old tradition at Longthorpe, that corpse candles would often arise out of the graves of those newly interred, and one old resident there who lived opposite the graveyard for some years, said that one night he distinctly saw three corpse candles rise out of the grave of a villager newly interred, and then disappear."

That fascinating writer on the North Kent marshes, who wrote under the *nom-de-plume* of "A Son of the Marshes", refers in several of his books to "corpse candles" being seen on the marshes in the neighbourhood of Milton-next-Sitting-bourne, some sixty or seventy years ago, but personally I am of the opinion that the Will-o'-the-Wisp, which actually exists, is something quite different from the alleged "corpse candles" which are said to arise from graves of the newly buried.

There is little doubt that Wills were seen as recently as 1939 on my own, then undrained, fen, a place of meres and steaming swamps in Burwell Fen, but nowadays, since it grows potatoes and corn, I should not expect to find one nearer than the Norfolk Broads. I must confess, however, that although I have rented several large tracts of Broadland marshes and know the district intimately, I have not yet had the luck to see one.

One of the best stories of a Norfolk Will, concerns the light known as "Neatishead Jack", the details of which were published in Volume II of *Norfolk Archaeology* from notes taken down by the Rev. John Gunn, of Irstead, from Mrs. Lubbock, of that parish, in 1849:

"Before the Irstead Enclosure in 1810 Jack-o'-Lantern was frequently seen here on a roky night, and almost always at a place called 'Heard's Hole' in Alder Carr Fen Broad on the Neatishead side, where a man of that name, who was guilty of some unmentionable crimes, was drowned. I have often seen it there, rising up and falling and twisting about and then up again. It looked exactly like a candle in a lantern."

She evidently connected the "ignis fatuus" in that spot with the unhappy man's spirit, as if it were still hovering about; and Jack-o'-Lantern was, in her apprehension, endued with volition and intelligence; for she affirms that if any one were walking along the road with a lantern, at the time when he appeared and did not put out the light immediately, Jack would come up against it and dash it to pieces; and that a gentleman who made a mock of him and called him "Will of the Wisp" was riding on horseback one evening in the adjoining parish of Horning, when he came at him and knocked him off his horse.

She remembers, when a child, hearing her father say that he was returning home from a large (largess) money-spending at the finish of harvest, in company with an old man, who whistled and jeered at Jack; but he followed them all the way home, and when they entered the house he torched up at the windows.

The Neatishead people were desirous to lay Heard's spirit, so annoyed were they by it; for it came at certain times and to certain places which he frequented when alive. Three gentlemen (she could not tell who or what they were, she supposed they

were learned) attempted to lay the ghost by reading verses of
Scripture. But he always kept a verse ahead of them. And they
could do nothing, till a boy brought a couple of pigeons and laid
them down before him. He looked at them and lost his verse;
and then they bound his spirit.

One of the best and most amusing accounts of a Norfolk
Lantern Man was given by the late Lady Cranworth, of
Letton, in an article she wrote for Volume I of the *Eastern
Counties Magazine,* in 1900, in which she said:

> Great interest gathers round the "Will-o'-the-Wisp" which
> seems to be very well known here, though I personally have never
> seen it. The local name for it—or him—is variously "Hob-o'-
> Lantern" or "The Lantern Man".
> We have an old horseman who has been with us for I should
> be afraid to say how many years. . . . He said with great scorn,
> "Ghosties! Who's a-believing in them? I've never seen naught
> and I've forgotten all the tales I heard about such nonsense. All
> I ever seed about the place—and I've been out rain and fine at all
> hours of the night—was the Lantern men. I've seen them scores
> of times running about. They fare to come out o' the ground and
> run about and around. They tell me they're wapers (vapours):
> I don't know!"
> These Lantern men are commonly supposed to be dangerous
> to life. "Folks du say that if one man stand at one end of the
> field and another man stand over agin him in the other corner,
> and they will whistle each to other, the Lantern man will always
> run to the whistle. It is a good thing to know this as the Lantern
> man will always try to come agin you and to kill ye, if so be he
> is able."
> A story which comes from Cromer illustrates further the danger
> of falling in with the Lantern Men and ends up with some sound
> advice as to the way of dealing with them in case of need. It is
> told by an old fisherman and runs thus:
> "There's no saying what that will du to you, if that light on
> you! There was a young fellow coming home one evening and he
> see the Lantern Man coming for him and he run; and that run!

and he run again; and that run again! Now there was a silly old man lived down there who didn't believe in none o' them things and this young fellow he run to his house and say, 'O Giles, for Heaven's sake, let me in—the Lantern Man's coming!' And old Giles he say, 'You silly fool, there ain't no such thing as a Lantern Man.' But when he see the Lantern Man coming for him, Giles let the young fellow in, and that come for them two, till that was the beginer of a pint pot!

"And old Giles, he thought he would play a trick on the Lantern Man so he got a candle and held that out of the window on the end of a pole. And fust he held that out right high; and the Lantern Man, he come for that and he come underneath it. And then he held that out right low and the Lantern Man he come up above it. And then he held that out right steady, and the Lantern Man he come for that and he burst it all to pieces.

"But they du say, if the Lantern Man light upon you, the best thing is to throw yourself flat on your face and hold your breath."

This obviously refers to the danger of breathing the marsh gas of which the Lantern Man is composed.

At Syleham, a parish in the upper reaches of the River Waveney, Wills-o'-the-Wisp were so common eighty or ninety years ago, that they were known as Syleham Lights, and the late W. A. Dutt, in that charming book *The Norfolk Broadland*, speaks of an old inn-keeper who had "heard tell" of a ball of flame which was seen to float across the marshes and then, when it reached the river, clung for a while to the mast of a wherry. This phenomenon has been recorded more than once in the past, and reminds one of the seamen's tales of corposants or St. Elmo's Fire, the balls of light which are sometimes seen on ships during storms.

The late Reverend Charles Kent, for many years a well-known parson in the Breckland district, referred to Wills-o'-the-Wisp in his book *The Land of the Babes in the Wood,* but said that, in his district, they were known as "Shiners" and were regarded with mortal terror by the villagers. I can only conclude that Mr. Kent's "Shiners" must have been seen on or about Tomston Water or Stanford Mere, the two great Breckland lakes on Lord Walsingham's estate which Charles Kent knew so well.

A writer in *Norfolk and Norwich Notes and Queries* on December 31st, 1904, had an amusing story to tell which confirms some old village beliefs that the harmless Will-o'-the-Wisp was a ferocious evil spirit that would attack a man on sight, although, in my native Fens, the legend is that the Will, instead of attacking, sought to lead one to a watery and ghastly grave in the deepest and smelliest part of the Fen— which would inevitably have happened had one been fool enough to follow it. That is the more general and sensible belief.

The writer in *Notes and Queries*, however, says:

Nobody ever sees the "Lantern Man" in these days, but in gran' pa's young days he was always about on the marshes on "roky" nights and many's the stout marshman who has attempted to follow him and found himself up to his knees in some treacherous swamp. Ordinary folks have heard of Jack-o'-Lanterns as a mere flickering light, pale and intangible and always far away. Not so the marshmen. Why, some of them have been followed by the fiery sprite, and when they got indoors have seen their windows lighted up by the thwarted bogie. Once a man was jogging homeward in the dark, carrying a lantern as a mild guide to his doubtful footsteps and Master Jack came out of the swamp and followed him! The man knew what to do. He just stood the lantern down and ran for all he was worth. When he turned round to look, there was Jack, kicking the lantern about with all the rage imaginable.

Christopher Davies, in *Norfolk Broads and Rivers,* mentioned seeing a Will-o'-the-Wisp frequently some seventy years ago. He quotes a wherryman as saying that he always fired his gun at them to put them out, for "if you did not fire at them, they were likely to come near you and do you some hurt". M. E. Walcott, in *The East Coast of England,* 1864, says of the Horning district, "Jack-o'-Lantern haunts these marshes and torments homeward bound farmers, knocking them down and dismounting them." That is obvious nonsense. The farmers had clearly made a night of it at the Ferry Inn, and fell off their horses with fright or were thrown when the animals reared on their hind-legs as any horse would do if one put a ball of fire under its nose. I like much better the story of the Horning Donkey, told by Suffling in *The Innocents on the Broads*, to wit:

I can't say as I've seen a human ghost, but I have seen the Horning ghost in the Long Lane—that's the ghost of a dickey (donkey) yer know.

I wuz coming from Walsham one night in the winter-time, and I don't know how it wuz, but suthin' fare tu say to me—"Look behind."

Well, I must, fule like, look roun', 'cause I fancied I could hear sumthin' go clickerty click, clickerty click, behind me. Sure nuff, there came a white dickey lopin' along the road, all alone. I felt a bit scart and my old hobby pricked up har lugs as much as to say "Hello, hu's this a follerin' me?" Presently I pulled up short like and the white dickey he pull up tu. Then when I go on, he go on, and w'en I stop, he stop. So thinks I, yew ain't no ghost anyhow. Then a bright idea cum inter me hid. "I'll go back and see who's donkey 'tis."

So I tarned round and back I go, and when I'd got almost up to the white dickey who stud right in the middle o' the road facin' me, my old hobby stopped short and nearly hulled me outer the cart. Poor ole girl she whinney'd wi' fright and roun' she came of her own accord and along the lane she go as hard as she could clap her fower huffs to the ground.

But it worn't no use; this here white dickey sune began to shorten the distance and every time I looked roun' it wuz nigher. Lord, I felt all of a muck sweat and I know me eyeballs stood out so that any one might ha' chopped 'em out wi' a hook. Closer it cum, and close; an' when I looked roun' agin, it wuz just behin' with smoke comin' outer its nosterels like out of a furnace, and I du believe there wuz a little pink flame with it, but thet I ain't

sure about, cuz I wuz upset. But this I du know the smell o'
sulphur was right powerful.

I pulled old Cally—short for California—inter the deek (dyke)
and past came this here white dickey and sure nuff it wuz a ghost
arter all, for I could see every bar of a gate by the rodeside rite
trew its maizey body.

My ha'r must 'av' riz on me hid, for orf went me hat. Away
went the dickey up the Long Lane leading past the church to the
village, and away went old Cally arter it, full tare, and think's I
wot's agoen to happen nixt.

Why it came to an ind like a flash. When the dickey come to
the churchyard wall it plumped trew it jest as easy as I could
poke my finger trew a pat of butter and wot's more it didn't
distarb a single stoon of the thick wall.

Yew may laff, but nex' mornin' when I went ter look for my
hat—'cause I dussen't goo back that night—I took a good view o'
the churchyard wall, and there worn't a hole in it nowhere, and
not a single print of a dickey's huff in the roadway.

At Ludham, that pleasant old marshland village on the
tortuous waters of the Ant, which is mainly notable for the
remains of a once-beautiful Old Hall, most of which was
burned down in 1611, they have the legend of the Ludham
Serpent. Now this mighty snake which terrorised the entire
parish, seems to have existed in actual fact, for in the *Norfolk
Chronicle* of September 28th, 1782, there appeared the
following:

On Monday the 14th inst. a snake of an enormous size was
destroyed at Ludham in this County by Jasper Andrews of that
place. It measured 5 feet 8 inches long, was almost 3 feet in
circumference and had a very long snout. What is remarkable
there were two excrescences on the forepart of the head which
very much resembled horns. The creature seldom made its
appearance in the day time but kept concealed in subterranean
retreats several of which have been discovered in the town, one
near the bake-office and another on the premises of the Revd.
N. V. Jeffrey and another in the land occupied by Mr. Popple at

the Hall. The skin of the above surprising reptile is now in the possession of Mr. J. Garrod, a wealthy farmer in the neighbourhood.

There is also a story, somewhat later in date, I think, of two snakes six feet long each, attacking a man at Dereham.

Female grass snakes, in marshy areas, not uncommonly grow to a length of 4 feet 6 inches—I killed one myself of that size in Wicken Fen—but the chances are that these serpents were foreigners which had escaped from ships that had docked at Yarmouth, and had made their way inland. A similar legend of a great snake which came out of Bulphan Fen, exists at Herongate in Essex, where it is said to have been slain by Sir John Tyrell of Heron Hall.

Sailors are notoriously superstitious, and coastal fishermen share most of their beliefs. I have spent many years of my life fishing and wildfowling on the eastern coasts of England, from the Isle of Harty on the Kentish Swale, a land of sheep and houseless marshes, to the wide and shining mud-flats of the Essex Blackwater, the manless stretches of the Norfolk coast and as far north as the haunted land of Holy Island, where Saint Columba lit the first faint lamp of Christianity in this realm.

One of the most remarkable first-hand ghost stories I ever heard was of a spectral Viking. It was told me in a wildfowler's hut built from the timbers of a stranded barge on Canvey Island, some twenty-five years ago. The teller was Charlie Stamp, the wildfowler and fisherman of Canvey Point, a mahogany-skinned, sharp-eyed little man, with gold earrings in his ears, as tough as old wire nails, and as full of salt-water wisdom as an oyster is of meat.

I have told the story in another book, *Coastal Adventure,* but I make no apology for telling it here again, as Charlie told it me that night, sitting in the semi-dark with the fire of ships' timbers sputtering blue and red as the flames got at the tar. It is one of the most astonishing stories of a ghost I

The Ghost of a Viking

have ever heard from any countryman, and, told that night, with the winter wind rattling the windows and the curlews crying on the mud-flats outside, it had an uncanny air of reality.

> I laid in me truckle bed lookin' out o' the winder of a midnight [said Charlie]. Bright moon that was, bright as day. An' I reckon I had a dream. I dreamt there was an owd feller come up over the saltin's, over the wall an' across the plank into my garden. A rum owd feller. He stood six foot. He had a leather jerkin on wi' a belt an' a sword and cross-garters below his knees. He had a funny owd hat on his head—like a helm that was, with wings on. An' long moustaches an' a beard.
>
> "I've lost me ship, mate," he say. "I want to get a ship back to me own country. I'm a lost man."
>
> "Goo you up to Grays or Tilbury," I says. "You'll get a ship there, mate, to carry you to any port in the world."
>
> He wagged his owd head an' looked at me right sorrowful. "I count I 'on't find no ship to take me to my port. I'm a lost man."
>
> An' he walked over that sea-wall, master, an' away out on the marsh, an' I never seed him no more.

Across the grey and misty estuary of the Thames, where Charlie has fished and fowled all his life, a buccaneer before the Lord, there lies the Isle of Sheppey, with the gaunt and ruined shell of the once-great Castle of Shurland, where lived the Lord of Shoreland, whom Parson Barham immortalised in his *Ingoldsby Legends*.

When I go fowling in the winter dusk on the sheep-walks of Sheppey, or the lower marshes of the little, lonely Isle of Harty, which is part of Sheppey, save when big tides flow, as they flowed in 1953, through the "low-ways" where once tall ships sailed, the marshmen tell me that, on nights of howling gale and lashing sea, you may see "Old Shoreland's lights" bobbing along the foreshore, following the edge of the hungry tide, seeking for the poor drowned and battered bodies of sailors cast ashore. And when the shelduck, that handsome half-goose, half-duck whom the marshmen call the bargoose or bargander, laughs his ghastly mirth far out in the channel, they say that it is the voice of drowned sailors mocking the living about to drown.

That almost forgotten chronicler of this Kentish half-land of the sea, "A Son of the Marshes", tells in one of his books of a wild night spent fowling with two fishermen on the mud-flats of the Swale when the gale howled, the sea groaned on the bar, and all night the sky was alive with the cries and whistles, the clanging and clamour of gulls and wild geese, ducks and waders, flighting restlessly over the yeasty waters. One of the fishermen turned to him and said:

> When we started I thought we should ha' had a job to load an' fire fast enough, but not a shot shall we git tonight or mornin' proper; the minster hev just banged out three o'clock. Them 'ere fowl won't come inshore, not a bit on it. Jest hear how restless they are hollerin'; I've heerd my father speak of the same thing arter a storm. There's a body o' some sort out over the bar wants to come in. An' the fowl knows it's out there; they've seen it, an' they won't settle till it comes ashore. If it don't, Shoreland's lights will be seen agin, lookin' for it all along foreshore.

The lights were said to be seen usually over a treacherous rotten swamp which lay just above high-water mark, and the belief was that the corpse candles were borne by the souls of those who had been drowned at sea and came ashore to hunt for a spot of dry ground, there to indicate to the living that they wished their bones to be laid when their bodies were washed ashore. If only the smallest remnant of a body could be found and given Christian burial, the ghost would be laid and the corpse candles put out. That belief still holds good today on Romney Marsh, round about the Reculvers, on Sheppey and on Swale, and on the lonely marshes of the Essex coast.

An old fisherman-gunner friend of mine, living now in that out-of-the-world village of Tollesbury at the mouth of the

Blackwater, a man who has sailed the Seven Seas in sail and has fowled all his life on his native mud-flats, refuses any longer to go to evening flight on the lonely spit known as the Naas End, because, he swears to me, that there walks at night, gun in hand, the ghost of an old friend of both of us, a great gentleman-gunner, who lies buried in Tollesbury churchyard.

Another native of Tollesbury, Mr. F. Garrod, who lives now in Welwyn Garden City, sends me, in a letter, a whole bevy of Tollesbury ghosts.

There was [he writes] supposed to have been a White Lady who walked in the road at the end of the drive to Gorwell Hall, where she is said to have had her throat cut. Another place supposed to be haunted is the Monk's House. It is said to have a tunnel leading to Tollesbury Church, but it probably stands on the site of an older house. The old Workhouse was another haunted place. These were a row of old, weather-boarded cottages down North Road, pulled down some years ago. As children we always used to run past these at night, for the ghost there used to smash the crocks and throw things about.

Another queer story current when I was a boy was that at certain times in the year the ghost of a white rabbit could be seen in the churchyard. There are other houses in the village supposed to be haunted, but these were the sort of common talk.

Going on to witches [he writes], this is rather a delicate subject, although interesting, because in my young days there were at least four people who were supposed to be witches, so you can imagine there are still some of their relatives alive!

The best story, I think, was of a fisherman whose mother was said to be a witch. One day he was out dredging (or "drudging" as they say) for oysters. He kept shooting his dredge, and each time he hauled it in, he could see that it had been on its back. About the fourth time he was so enraged, that he swore and cursed about his old mother for bewitching him. He picked the dredge up, and tore the "rigging" (this is the net part) to pieces with his teeth, and threw it down on the deck with such force that it bounced up and went down the cabin hatch.

The funny thing was, that try as he would, he could not get it up again, and he had to cut it with a cold chisel and hammer, as this was the days before they carried hacksaws aboard smacks. Incidentally this man used to go every Sunday to Chapel with a big Bible under his arm.

The other three witches included a travelling gipsy and two local women. I was forbidden by my aunt to even look at the house where one of them lived. I have known people to put a piece of their toenail and a wisp of hair from the person who had cast a spell on them, into the fire, whilst at the same time the poker was put in and lifted when it was red hot. This they called "branding the witch" and breaking the spell.

They swore you could see the marks on the witches body after this performance.

My correspondent ends by saying, "I hope you will be able to make something of this scriven"—here he uses a charming, but alas obsolete, old English word—"but anything I can do to help you with the book, will be a pleasure if any use."

Such beliefs, scoffed at by pseudo-scientific minds, are too deep-rooted for the countryman to ignore, too interesting to be lost. On the other hand, many of the country beliefs in ghostly lights and hauntings, particularly on the coast, were either started or fostered by smugglers, as an admirable means of keeping other people's noses out of their midnight business. There was little or no deliberate "wrecking" on the East coast, of the sort which made the Cornish, Devon, and Irish coasts notorious, because there are no rocks on which you can wreck a ship, and any vessel which goes ashore, generally does so a long way from land, either on a sandbank or a mud-flat. On the other hand, smuggling was rampant, and still goes on, to a certain extent, to this day. The deserted and tortuous coastal creeks of the Kent and Essex shores, where, nowadays, you may walk for a week without seeing a coastguard, are ideal for the purpose.

A good picture of what conditions were like a hundred

years ago, in the Rochford Hundred of Essex, which includes the desolate islands of Foulness, Potton, Wallasea, Rushley, Havengore, and New England, is given by Philip Benton, of Wakering Hall, who writing in 1868 says:

> With respect to the Clergy, it is notorious the majority, for more than two centuries, were noted for their incompetence, their vices, and shameful neglect of their duties. At the period to which we are now alluding, in the twenty-seven parishes there were not above three to five resident beneficed men, and those upon the poorest Livings, whilst the Curates had charge of three, four, or even five churches. Their stipends were shameful, and their characters had little to recommend them.
>
> Within the present century, taking some half-dozen contiguous parishes we gather, principally from records, that one Vicar S.— who dabbled in farming, and made a granary of the parsonage, used to drive his pigs to Rochford Market, dressed in a blue frock-coat, red comforter, and velveteen breeches, and to stop at The Three Ashes to drink on his way.
>
> He once carried on this dialogue in Church, tapping the Clerk on his shoulder: Vicar, "Is my boy Jack in Church?" Clerk, "No." Vicar, after a time, "Is my boy, etc., etc.?" "Confound it, I shan't have a cherry on my tree when I get back. . . ."
>
> It may be easily supposed at this period that superstition reigned supreme over weak and credulous minds, when the schoolmaster had made little or no progress, and that belief in ghost-seeing and witchcraft was prevalent amongst all classes, and incredible stories with a perfect belief in their truth are told about haunted houses and lanes.

Harriott, another local historian, relates how a poor elderly woman waited upon him, complaining that her neighbours accused her of being a witch, and that she had teats in her armpits with which she suckled young imps, and requesting him to examine her, and certify if it were so or not. Many lanes had their "black dog".

Rochford Hall, the old Essex home of Anne Boleyn's family, a hundred and seventy years ago had a very lively ghost. In a letter written by the Rev. Nicholas Griffinhoofe, rector of Woodham Mortimer, in August 1776, he says:

> The Rochford Hall Ghost grows more rude every day. He now amuses himself with throwing the boots and shoes at the men's heads. Mr. Wright was at Rochford the week before last, and sent in a great hurry for Mr. Codd and me to come to exorcise this riotous Ghost, but I was unluckily in Town.

Writing again in September, he says:

> The ghost still continues to molest the good folks at Rochford Hall, but he will not dare to make his appearance this week, as a large body of men, women, and children are set off for Rochford Hall on Wednesday next, Mr. and Mrs. Codd and their daughter Fanny; Mr. and Mrs. Williams, of Maldon; Mr. and Mrs. Griff and their daughter Sofey, are to form the cavalcade, but the chief business of this expedition is to eat fruit of all kinds, as there is great plenty of it there; we propose staying two or three days, and I daresay the ghost will remain very quiet all the time we are there.

For some years I rented the shooting on Potton Island and later on Wallasea Island, both near Rochford, and I heard at first hand many stories and beliefs in witches and wise men. The little village of Canewdon, perched on an upland overlooking the salt-water estuary of the Crouch was, within living memory, a very nest of witches. The butcher's wife and the parson's wife were said to be two of them. Witch Hart was one of the most famous. It is said of her that she stole one of the church bells out of Canewdon Church and sailed down the Crouch in it. Another poor old lady at Fambridge, a little higher up the river, suspected of being a witch, was taken out in a boat, her thumbs and toes tied together and she was then "hulled overboard" into salt water, to see if she would sink or float. But for the intervention of one or two stout-hearted people, who, defying the witch-hunters, hauled her aboard their boat, she would undoubtedly have been drowned.

My old friend, the late Will Goodchild, a splendid type of Essex yeoman, who lived at East Horndon Hall until his death in 1952, owned the whole of Wallasea Island within recent years. He often told me that Devil's House, a ramshackle farmhouse at the far end of the island, whose bedroom windows peered over the sea-wall towards the flat and almost treeless wastes of Foulness Island, was supposed to be haunted by the Devil.

"Some nights," Will said, "the cattle in the stockyards seem to go mad. They stampede about as though the Devil were after them. And my old chap says that He is there, stirring them up with his fork!"

It is certainly true that one night in 1938 a mob of cattle which had been rounded up in the stockyard, charged the gates, knocked them flat and stampeded wildly all over the marsh. In the great tidal flood of 1953, the whole of Wallasea Island was flooded, some of it thirteen feet below salt water, and the remains of Devil's House or Tile Barn and other farmhouses, were levelled flat by the battering of the waves.

Perhaps that is as well, for Alfred Herbert Martin, an old farm labourer who has worked on the islands for over forty years told me, only a few years ago, that when he and another labourer were sleeping upstairs in Devil's House, the Devil came after them in person. Here is the story in Alfred's own words:

Same as that owd Davvle's house. I know'd that well tharty year agoo. An owd thatched place with a rare gret owd barn—suffin' lonely, I tell yer. I bided a week there. One night my mate found hisself hulled out o' bed an' down the stairs. He never know'd what done it. That owd davvle wore strong as a hoss.

Tew nights arterward he rowed over to Foulness Island across the creek. He come back late in the moonlight, bright as day that wore.

"Alf," he say to me, "what do you reckon I seed when I was a-rowin' acrost the crick? I seed that owd Mrs. Smith, owd

Mother Redcap, from Foulness, comin' acrost the water on a wooden hurdle in the moonlight. She dedn't hev no oars, but she travelled same as if she was in a boat. She's the headest witch about these parts. You look out, bor! She's on this island somewhere now."

An, yu believe me, sir, when we looked in the barn next mornin' there was that owd witch curled up in the straw like a cat! She come in the house, 'cause we had her son workin' along wi' us, an' I mind her well, settin' by the fire, peelin' pertaters, nippin' her owd lips tergither, an' a-mumblin': "Holly, Holly! Brolly, Brolly! Redcap! Bonny, Bonny!"

Blast, boy, she scat me! There was several witches them days, but that owd Mother Redcap was the headest one o' the lot. I got out o' Davvle's House suffin' quick arter that.

Well, that is Alfred's story, and, wagging the gold earrings in his ears, and puffing Niggerhead smoke into my face, he assured me with the utmost solemnity: "Thass a true piece, master. True as I set here. An' if that ain't true, may th'owd Davvle fly away with me. I on'y hope th'owd humbug had to swim for it the night the tide bruk in!"

After such a declaration of faith, who are we to cavil?